SHREVEPORT'S
HISTORIC GREENWOOD CEMETERY

ECHOES IN GRANITE AND MARBLE

GARY D. JOINER, PhD

THE
History
PRESS

Published by The History Press
Charleston, SC
www.historypress.com

First published 2023

Manufactured in the United States

ISBN 9781467152402

Library of Congress Control Number: 2022944978

To
Laura Claire Nations
and
Mary Rachel Schlidt,
My daughter and granddaughter.
I could not be prouder of both of you.

Lord, help me dig into the past
And sift the sands of time,
That I might find the roots that made
This family tree of mine.

Lord, help me trace the ancient roads
On which my fathers trod,
And led them through so many lands
To find our present sod.

Lord, help me find an ancient book
Or dusty manuscript,
That's safely hidden now away
In some forgotten crypt.

Lord, let it bridge the gap that haunts
My soul when I can't find,
The missing link between some name
That ends the same as mine.

—Author Unknown

CONTENTS

LIST OF IMAGES

TOUR STOPS IN
GREENWOOD CEMETERY

23	J.C. Willis
24	A.C. Steere
25	Ida Chapman
26	D.B. Napier
27	LSU Medical School
28	Willa Norwood
29	Burch Grabill
30	Laura May Ferguson
31	Wheless Family
32	R.W. Norton Family
33	Baby Boy Villarreal
34	Charles Dunn
35	Lefty Leonardos
36	Bush Kile Jarratt
37	Sam C. Caldwell
38	Martha Nabors
39	Michael Roach
40	Marie Curtis
41	Ellerbe Family
42	Joe Family
43	Dessie Alberta Martin
44	William B. Wiener
45	Harold and Carolyn Murov
46	Larry Planchard and Nancy Planchard
47	Bruno and Bertha Strauss
48	Rabbi David Lefkowitz Jr.

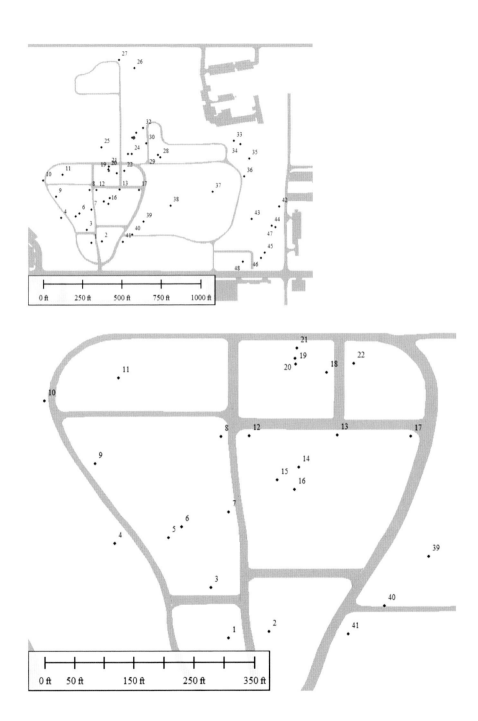

GLOSSARY OF TERMS

bas relief: Incised decoration, a carved incision below a background plane.

cenotaph: A large headstone inscribed with the family's name to whom the plot belongs. A family name marker does not indicate a burial; it only indicates a family plot.

columbarium: A room, building or wall with niches for storing funeral urns.

column: A single pillar standing alone as a monument, usually surmounting a pedestal or pedestal base.

cruciform (cross): A cross, with or without inscription, placed in the ground or supported by a pedestal.

epitaph: A phrase or longer passage written in memory of a person who has died, especially on a tombstone.

ferns: Define the life of the person representing sincerity, humility or solitude.

granite: A hard igneous crystalline rock consisting of small, visible amounts of other materials. Usually red, pink or gray variegated.

ground tablet: An inscribed marker laid flush with or slightly above ground level.

headstone: An upright slab embedded in the ground or in a separate stone base and that is inscribed.

iconography: Artwork on a gravestone or other burial device, images or symbols that describe the deceased.

marble: A metamorphic stone, white or variously colored, sometimes streaked or mottled. Can be highly polished. Usually white and crystalline, although sometimes pink.

mausoleum: A tomb with accessible interior space, often containing wall or subterranean vaults and a small area intended for private prayer or contemplation accessed by a door (see Schumpert, Hancock).

obelisk: A monumental, four-sided stone shaft, usually monolithic and tapering to a pyramidal tip, that stands on a pedestal.

scroll: A representation of the book of life, the deeds accomplished and the final accounting of the individual.

sphere: An orb representing the world, unity or perfection.

tomb: A mortuary structure associated with or containing one or more burial vaults (see Atkins tomb).

tree stone: A marker carved in the shape of a tree stump, wood stack or a cross made of tree stumps and limbs, often including an inscription and a Woodmen of the World emblem.

ACKNOWLEDGEMENTS

All historians love working on projects such as this—perhaps not always the history of cemeteries, but major topics within their fields of study. Gathering tens of thousands of individual facts and dates, burial records, maps, city ordinances and resolutions, newspaper accounts and family histories takes time and patience. Before writing a book, thousands of hours of research and editing must occur. I am fortunate to work with the best graduate students, governmental stewards of precious records, archivists and librarians and professional researchers and friends who are all taphophiles. We love cemeteries. The Greenwood Cemetery project evolved over three years. This book covers a fraction of the graves in Greenwood.

Susan Hardtner of the Shreveport Garden Study Club contacted me about writing a book on Greenwood Cemetery. She is the epitome of the servant-leader. She and the club members offer a wealth of information. They partner with the Shreveport Public Assembly and Recreation (SPAR) Department of the City of Shreveport to improve the landscape of Greenwood and assist in maintaining its heritage. Shelly Ragle, the director of SPAR, is a faithful steward of the public's trust. She is responsible for the three large public cemeteries in Shreveport, keeping the parks open and the public spaces mowed and running recreational programs. She loves history too.

Joanna Hunt and Julianna Horrell are among the best graduate student researchers with whom I am honored to work at Louisiana State University–Shreveport. They help with the research portion of the project firsthand, helping see how documents fit together.

The Northwestern Louisiana Archives at LSU-Shreveport is home for the City of Shreveport records beginning in the late 1830s, coroners' files, arrest blotters, newspaper stories and photography and private photographers' images, among other treasures. Domenica Carriere is as much a sleuth as any historian, and she knows where to find where the best information is located.

John Andrew Prime was a newspaper reporter and editor for many years. He is a tremendous resource and has a penchant for finding arcane facts. I am proud to have him as a friend and collaborator.

The late Eric Brock and I worked on many local and regional history projects before his untimely death. Eric's widow, Shannon Glasheen Brock, is a fine researcher in her own right and is very much a part of this book. Their contributions were essential.

Finally, but certainly not least, my wife, Marilyn Segura Joiner, is my partner, editor extraordinaire, fellow historian and researcher and the love of my life (not in that order). She puts up with my research needs and is always ready to assist in my projects.

INTRODUCTION

Shreveport, Louisiana, is home to several large cemeteries, each with a complex history and most with beautiful statuary or monuments. The city's first municipal cemetery was Oakland, located on the western edge of downtown. Oakland served Shreveport's needs until the great yellow fever epidemic in 1873 and several decades later. Fully one-quarter of the city's population perished in the epidemic. Before 1873, it was clear that Oakland could not be expanded due to urbanization. After several attempts to find a suitable successor, in 1893, Shreveport purchased a twenty-acre parcel on the north side of Stoner Avenue at the end of Market Street. The city added land until the cemetery grounds were completed in 1912. Greenwood Cemetery consists of over seventy acres and at least twenty thousand graves.

Greenwood was a hospital site before and during the Civil War and a tuberculosis facility called the "pest house" before the current cemetery was dedicated. At least 150 Confederates treated at the hospital died and have no permanent markers. Following the Battles of Mansfield and Pleasant Hill in 1864, many Union dead were buried among their foes after dying from their injuries. Perhaps hundreds of patients who died of consumption (tuberculosis) were buried without a permanent memorial. These burials are on the high ground in the northwest corner of the cemetery, in the low area now under the pond and along both sides of the western boundary fence. All of these burials, if marked, used wooden planks that have long since disintegrated.

The oldest burials in Greenwood predate the Civil War. These African Americans were enslaved people on the Stoner Plantation, which stretched from Market Street, east to Clyde Fant Parkway and then south to Shreveport-Barksdale Highway. The area is still called Stoner Hill. The burials are located on the east side of the cemetery and east of the St. George Greek Cemetery section. Later, members of the Stoner Hill Baptist Church were buried there. Many graves are marked, but it is important to recognize that this large open grass area contains many burials, unidentified and known only to God.

Oakland Cemetery began during the formative years of the American rural cemetery movement. Greenwood was surveyed near its end. The oldest streets in Greenwood curve in gentle arcs, and only in later expansions do they form straight lines and sharp intersections. Following the custom of the movement, most of the cemetery is laid out in a haphazard design. Formal blocks do not always exist in a logical order, and some dedicated block numbers were not used in the cemetery. Greenwood has eighty-one numbered blocks, but only seventy-four exist.

Additionally, some surveyed areas do not have formal block numbers. Perhaps Greenwood's most important layout scheme is the system of "rests," of which there are thirty-six. Some of these are called sections, but they all share a common theme. Each rest is the burial area of a group. Visitors will find two Masonic rests; a Confederate Veterans' Bivouac; rests for five formal trade unions; one for Greek Orthodox burials; one for the B'nai Zion congregation; one each for the Independent Order of Odd Fellows, the Knights of Pythias and the Ascension Commandery of the Knights Templar; one for infants; separate rests for veterans of the Spanish-American War and World War I; and a combined area for the Veterans of Foreign Wars, the American Legion and the Disabled American Veterans. One rest is for the Genevieve Orphanage. Another is dedicated to Shreveport firefighters who died in the line of service.

Greenwood also contains areas that speak to compassion for the homeless, the derelict and people who could not afford a typical burial. The first rest dedicated in Greenwood was the Potters' Field. In the northern half of the cemetery are three rests called "payrows" or "pay rows." These sections contain burials of families who paid the sexton to open and close the grave, but there was no formal service. Instead, sites were picked by the next available with no family plots. Some of these are marked, but many are not.

Visitors to Greenwood are often drawn to the magnificent architecture of tombs and mausoleums. Three large structures stand out near the main entrance gate. Dr. T.E. Schumpert's mausoleum and the Atkins family crypt are topped with magnificent angels. The Hancock mausoleum contains a large pillar on the roof. All three were built in a style that dates back to the ancient Persian empire. Near these are obelisks, columns, spheres, cylinders, Celtic crosses and intricately carved monuments called tree stones. Veterans' rests vary from individual family monuments to standard military-issue marble headstones dating from the period of the individual's service, not their date of death. These markers form orderly ranks and files. A group of unobtrusive, low monuments is found in Babyland. There is no order behind the beautiful iron gate. The graves are for stillborns and infants, and they were buried eclectically. Many graves are elaborately decorated, while others are "folk stones" placed by family members who still honor their deceased children.

Greenwood Cemetery exists in its present form thanks to a cooperative agreement between the City of Shreveport and the Shreveport Garden Study Club. The latter has worked tirelessly creating projects such as a pavilion overlooking the ravine that is now dammed and a water feature that greets visitors. They have created overlooks and places for visitors to rest and enjoy the landscaping. Through its Shreveport Public Assembly and Recreation Department, the city and the Garden Study Club combined efforts to create period-like street signage. SPAR ensures that the lawns are mowed, and the parklike setting beckons the visitor back to the turn of the twentieth century.

Both Oakland and Greenwood Cemeteries are crown jewels of Shreveport. They are social laboratories that help us know who was here, what they did and what their families wish people to remember about them. In Greenwood, visitors can find heroes and villains, mayors, bankers, industrialists, the well-to-do and the forgotten. A few of their stories are included in this book. Enjoy the stories and the artwork. Take some time to stroll through Greenwood and learn about those who came before us.

A HISTORY AND TOUR
OF GREENWOOD CEMETERY

Greenwood Cemetery is the largest public cemetery in Shreveport, Louisiana, comprising approximately seventy acres. Lying west and south of Youree Drive, it is the resting place of mayors, war heroes, wealthy planters and merchants, tens of thousands of ordinary folks and more than a few villains. Greenwood came into existence in the 1890s as Oakland Cemetery, located west of downtown, neared capacity. Greenwood remains active today, but with far fewer new burials. The parklike setting with beautiful trees and shrubs and broadly curving streets with names like Acacia, Beryl, Garnet and Oleander indicate that Greenwood began at the end of the Romanticism era's rural cemetery movement.[1] The cemetery features gently rolling terrain on a ridge west of the Red River, with the northern portion dropping away in steep slopes.

Shreveport began as a frontier town in 1839 and was, during its formative years, the westernmost municipality in the United States. Downtown Shreveport occupies a roughly one-square-mile diamond-shaped plateau that drops steeply on its south and western sides. The downtown plateau offered many amenities, but space for a municipal cemetery was not one of them. Shreveport opened its city cemetery, Oakland Cemetery, in 1847 near the western edge of downtown. The nine-acre cemetery covering four city blocks appeared to have plenty of room for the future.

Immediately south of downtown is a valley that runs east–west. The southeastern portion of this valley was the bed of a shallow body of water known as Silver Lake. The lake was very shallow during the Civil War, perhaps no more than one foot deep. Greenwood Cemetery lies on a high plateau south of downtown and across Silver Lake from the commercial district. Since Shreveport's incorporation, the ridge was deeply rural, with cotton fields and pastures, and it remained outside the city limits for more than fifty years. The high ground from Market Street west to Clyde Fant Memorial Parkway and then south to Shreveport-Barksdale Highway formed the Stoner Plantation, named for Samuel W. Stoner. It is known as Stoner Hill today.[2]

Shreveport in 1860 was a prosperous, tough town. The population was 2,190.[3] As the South moved toward the Civil War, Louisianans responded. As the war progressed from 1861 to 1863, Shreveport found itself as the capital of Confederate Louisiana and headquarters of the Army of the Trans-Mississippi (or the Army of Western Louisiana). Confederate engineers created fortifications in a vast arc from the hills above Red River at Stoner Avenue, extending west and exploiting the high ground. Then it ran northwest, then north, to a high point above Cross Bayou.[4] The fortifications consisted of four primary forts and fourteen imposing artillery forts on both sides of the river in Shreveport and what is today Bossier City. The Shreveport forts were connected by a series of earthen berm walls except where ravines made them impractical.[5] In addition, the engineers created a navy yard on Cross Bayou as local and regional industries expanded to assist the war effort. This activity made Shreveport a target for the Union forces in 1864.[6]

The southeast anchor of the inner defenses was an imposing fortification named Fort Turnbull, but it was locally called Fort Humbug due to its lack of cannons. The southern line of forts and walls extended west through what is today Greenwood Cemetery from this fort. Battery 3 was at the eastern edge of the cemetery. A bronze marker shows the approximate location in the St. George Greek Orthodox section, east of the curve of Acacia Drive.

Battery IV stood on the later Confederate Veterans' Bivouac. It is also marked with a bronze marker. These batteries faced south, but the guns could turn to the northeast to fire on any Union gunboats attempting to attack Shreveport.[7] The defensive wall linked the batteries and ran east–west about thirty feet south of Acacia Drive. A supply road ran behind and parallel to the defensive wall. Outside and east of the cemetery, the road had a shed roof, labeled "Covered Road" on the map.[8] The covered portion did not extend into the graveyard.

The southernmost and highest portion of a steep wagon road ran roughly parallel to the Caddo Juvenile Court complex between the Veterans of Foreign

Above: A portion of the Venable Map. Batteries 3 and 4 are in Greenwood Cemetery. *Northwest Louisiana Archives at LSU-Shreveport.*

Left: Artillery Battery 3 marker. *Image by the author.*

25

Wars section and Masons' Rest. This road served the cotton plantations to the south and formed an interior line of communication with both the Red River and Silver Lake during the Civil War. It descends from 240 feet mean sea level (MSL) to 192 feet in the old Cotton Belt Railroad (current Union Pacific Railroad) bed on the floor of Silver Lake.[9] Unfortunately, the creation and expansion of Youree Drive destroyed the middle portion of this road, but the steep incline from Youree Drive up to the cemetery remains. There are identifiable graves along the road and at the upper end.[10]

The end of the Civil War brought Shreveport prosperity, even during the early dark days of the Reconstruction era. The town did not see the ravages of battles, sieges or malicious burning, as did Alexandria in central Louisiana. The Army of the Trans-Mississippi was the last Confederate field army to disband, and its members could and did boast that it was the only Confederate army not to suffer defeat in battle.[11] Most of its leaders were from Louisiana and Texas and stayed there after the war. For the next five decades, most of Shreveport's leaders were Confederate veterans, significantly impacting the town and Greenwood Cemetery.

Oakland Cemetery was affected by Shreveport's growth. Workers who could not afford to live downtown rented shotgun houses in St. Paul's Bottoms, and Oakland was quickly surrounded by dense housing. As a result, Shreveport began searching for a new municipal cemetery. The earliest mention of this search is in the Shreveport City Council minutes of December 1, 1869. The council appointed a committee "for the purpose of

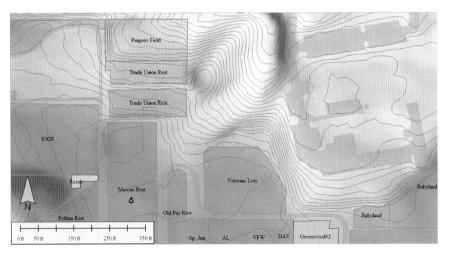

Map of the northern portion of Greenwood Cemetery showing the interior wagon road. *Cartography by Gary D. Joiner.*

locating [a] new Grave Yard."[12] The following year, the U.S. census showed the population of Shreveport was 4,607.[13] Shreveport became a city in 1871 with a former Confederate, Jerome B. Gilmore, as mayor.[14] The city council committee to find a new cemetery was not in a rush to perform their duty. Oakland still had plenty of room.

Medical facilities existed in Shreveport before the Civil War. The Confederates operated at least two facilities, one northwest of downtown and another called the Confederate and Marine Hospital, to the immediate west of Greenwood Cemetery. During and following the Red River Campaign of 1864, wounded Confederates and Union soldiers were treated at this facility. A list of Confederates who died at this hospital contains 149 named individuals, the units they served and the dates of their deaths. The notation on the list reads, "Most of these soldiers are buried in unmarked graves in Greenwood Cemetery, Shreveport."[15] These men were buried on both sides of the current boundary fence (which did not exist for another thirty years) and in what is now the northwest corner of the cemetery.

Additionally, like many other nineteenth-century cities, Shreveport suffered from persistent cases of consumption or tuberculosis. This highly contagious disease required quarantining, and patients were kept separately from the primary hospital building in a "pest house."[16] The cause of the disease was unknown, but it was greatly feared. The pest house was in the low area on the west side of Greenwood, where the pond is today. Those who died were buried amid the Confederate dead, with some later victims buried in the ravine.

Shreveport settled into life during Reconstruction. The U.S. Army Corps of Engineers based a unit on the Red River to remove the giant logjam called the "Great Raft." The U.S. Army headquarters in northern Louisiana was also based in Shreveport, enforcing the law with infantry and cavalry units. Although tension during the occupation existed, businesses opened, and the city made expansion plans. The mayor and the city council ordered the city surveyor, William R. DeVoe, to create the first detailed survey of the town and adjacent areas to prepare for future annexations.[17]

Stoner Plantation appears on this map to the southern limits of Township 18 North, Range 13 West. The eastern portion, in Section 32, remained under William Stoner's ownership. It contains a beef packery, a soap factory and a nursery.[18] Joseph B. Smith owned the area in Section 31. Although DeVoe laid out future blocks west of a proposed extension of Market Street, it remained undeveloped.

Shreveport experienced a seminal event in 1873, one that changed the course of its history for many decades to come. Beginning in mid-August and continuing through mid-November, the city suffered the third-greatest epidemic per capita of yellow fever in American history. Only the 1878 epidemics in Memphis and New Orleans were worse. People who could leave before the quarantine did so quickly. One-quarter of the population died, and a full half contracted "Yellow Jack" but lived. Shreveport could not keep up with what eventually became approximately 1,200 deaths. The city sexton dug trenches on the highest hill in Oakland, and wagonloads of bodies made their way from homes in the city to the cemetery. Ministers performed few religious services, and sextons buried bodies like cordwood.[19]

Following the epidemic, Shreveport began looking in earnest for another cemetery. The city committed to buying a tract from the Alston family that was located at the northeast corner of today's Lakeshore Drive and North Hearne Avenue.[20] Several charitable and fraternal orders wished to have plots when the land became available. The Independent Order of Odd Fellows, the Sons of Temperance, the B'nai Zion congregation and the Benevolent Association of Confederate Veterans requested dedicated areas.[21] The most significant demand for burial space was for paupers. Two acres were fenced with wire to accommodate this need.[22] Folks in Shreveport thought the distance to the graveyard was too far and the ride or drive to be inconvenient. Today, that site is unrecognizable. Graves are lost, and the surface has been strip-mined for sand and clay for road construction.

The city council looked for another alternative, and William DeVoe's map from 1873 became the primary reference source. The best option for a new cemetery was at the southern end of Market Street. Joseph Smith had conveyed his property in Section 31, Township 18 North, Range 13 West, south of Silver Lake to C.W. VanHoose and Ella V. Tomkies. The city records are vague, but it appears that Van Hoose and Tomkies sold twenty acres to the city for a cemetery on September 14, 1893 (the city council vote occurred on December 9, 1892).[23] The original plot was the south half, of the south half, of the west half, of the southeast quarter of Section 31. William DeVoe surveyed the new cemetery, laid out the streets and created blocks and lots within the blocks.[24]

Civic groups, trade unions and fraternal and charitable organizations requested blocks for their members to be buried together in dedicated sections called "rests."[25] Some of the rests co-opted designated blocks. Eventually, 35 rests were dedicated. The smallest is a single lot, and the largest contains 389 lots or plots. Commonly, several graves are found in a single-family plot.

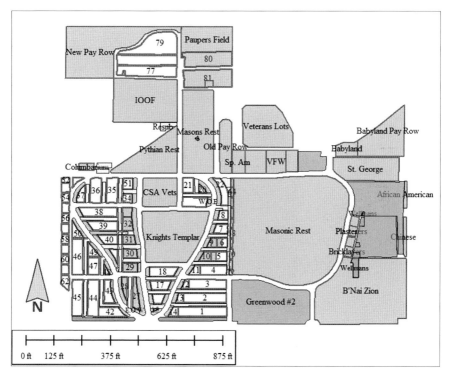

Map of Greenwood Cemetery showing blocks and rests. *Cartography by Gary D. Joiner.*

From the beginning of the cemetery, the city council decided that Greenwood should be orderly. Using DeVoe's original design, the curved streets and blocks would conform to the high land and be aesthetically pleasing.[26] Unlike Oakland, no families were allowed to erect interior fences regardless of the material or how ornate.[27] Street intersections would be marked with a stone engraved with the street names. (None exist, and the order may not have been carried out.)[28] A boundary fence was ordered from Stewart Brothers Ironworks in Cincinnati, Ohio.[29] The same firm created the ornate gate and boundary fence at Oakland. The existing fence along Stoner Avenue is from this order. Train car loads of gravel, used as a road base, were ordered for St. Joseph's Cemetery, Oakland Cemetery and Greenwood Cemetery.[30] The city council forbade the desecration of graves or the removal of flowers for other purposes.[31] Plot curbs must be no higher than fifteen inches and be constructed from concrete or other approved materials.[32] Greenwood was designated a wild bird sanctuary, with feeders and watering fountains built.[33] Many other actions kept the cemetery well drained, roads in proper shape and land acquired as needed.

As Greenwood grew to its present size, more acreage was needed for burials within the cemetery, and some dedicated streets were never built. These can often be determined by examining areas with two parallel sidewalks and grave lots between and adjacent to them. The city also took burial lot–sized strips adjoining the streets that were built and sold the small rights-of-way. The inconsistent numbering of sections is due to this awkward manner of creating more burial space. Adjoining blocks might have neighbors that have nothing to do with a logical numbering system. Today, there are seventy-four blocks from a total of eighty-one designated. There are no longer blocks 23, 24, 25, 26, 73, 74, 75 or 76, but there are two blocks 63. Except for blocks 77 through 81, all numbered blocks are located within the original twenty-acre parcel. Additionally, unnumbered portions of the cemetery not found in rests were plotted as part of an expansion called Greenwood No. 2. These are found throughout the cemetery.

The eclectic nature of Greenwood adds to its charm, if not an exceptionally disciplined concept. Majestic mausoleums are often adjacent to ground tablets that are flat and resistant to damage from mowers. Towering obelisks and columns are interspersed with Masonic tree stones, spheres, intricately carved granite and marble monuments, angels of various sizes, cenotaphs, benches and rows of veterans' markers, each in orderly ranks. Paupers' graves, primarily unmarked, lie near sections where families could only afford to bury their loved ones but not have a typical funeral. The road system within Greenwood, with its curved streets, is often confusing to navigate, but the elegant black street signs assist. As one walks or drives through the cemetery, finding a prominent mausoleum or other feature to use as a navigation aid is worthwhile. The best method to allow a thorough tour of Greenwood is to identify rests. This study will follow the rests in the rough order in which the cemetery was created and expanded. Some notable graves are not located in rests, and these should not be ignored. Later, some prominent individuals, their grave sites and monuments are discussed.

TOUR 1. THE ORIGINAL CEMETERY

Begin with the oldest portion of Greenwood, the original cemetery, which encompasses twenty acres that originate at the main entrance. The southern boundary line is Stoner Avenue. The western line is the western boundary fence. The northern line is Miriam Avenue. The eastern line is more difficult to distinguish.

As you walk or drive a short distance to the east of the intersection of Miriam and Eastern Avenues, you will note that Miriam Avenue becomes Acacia Drive. Here the cemetery plots are narrow and tightly aligned. Some ninety feet east of the corner, the plots are square. This is the boundary between the original portion of the cemetery and the newer Masonic Rest.

What to See

The gatehouse is to the left. A map of the cemetery is included there as a handy reference tool. Note as you enter that three streets diverge. Western Avenue is to your left, Eastern Avenue is to your right and straight ahead in the middle is Central Avenue. All form a loop with the top portion, which is named Miriam Avenue. They are intersected by Garnet, Turquoise, Beryl and Topaz Streets. An additional street, Oleander Avenue, begins at Turquoise and extends north.

Block 28

Starting at Western Avenue, immediately on the right, is Block 28, bounded by Western, Beryl Street and Central Avenue. Except for the African American burials on the cemetery's eastern edge, this contains the oldest burials. Graves in Block 28 were generally reinterred from Oakland Cemetery. These composed an unnamed rest. On the left are blocks 42 through 45. Across C Street (one of the many streets that were not finished but easily recognized) are blocks 46 through 50. Many early Masonic graves are here, and they exhibit some of the most delicate stone carving in the cemetery. However, this is not a Masonic rest. Facing east from the earliest burials in Block 28, you see the back of the imposing Schumpert mausoleum with an ornate angel seated on the roof.[34] The angel is an excellent navigation aid.

Blocks 29–33

Beginning at Beryl Street, turn left on Central Avenue. To your left is Planters' Row. Many of Shreveport's wealthy citizens lie here. On the north side of Beryl Street is the mausoleum of the Hancock family, whose story is tragic. The Hancocks moved the structure here from their backyard.

Blocks 38–40

A triangular segment of the cemetery lies here, immediately west of Planters' Row. These are attractive blocks, and the plots are aligned to conform to a street that was never built. Walking through the interior of this section, you see markers for Jean Despujols, the internationally famous artist; Reverend Robert James Harp; and William Kennon Henderson Jr., an industrialist turned media mogul.

Ascension Commandery, Knights Templar Rest

Just across Central Avenue, east of Planters' Row, is the intricately organized Ascension Commandery, Knights Templar Rest. The grid of plots maintains an east–west orientation, but the north side tilts to the northeast, making each lot a parallelogram. The dominant feature of this rest is the Atkins family mausoleum, imposing with its brilliant white marble and gray stone. The striking standing angel on the roof is the most delicate artwork in Greenwood Cemetery. Walking through the interior of this rest, you see markers for L. Calhoun Allen, one of the most influential mayors in Shreveport history; Dr. William Tucker Dalzell, a prototype of the servant-leader and hero of the yellow fever epidemic of 1873; Governor Newton Crain Blanchard (located midway along Turquoise Street, whose massive column designates the grave site of him, his wife and their son), a remarkable man who helped lead Louisiana out of the Gilded Age and into the progressive era; and J. Fair Hardin, a colonel in the army, commanding Fort Humbug Armory, assistant U.S. attorney, federal prosecutor, Mason and the author of the seminal history of northwestern Louisiana.

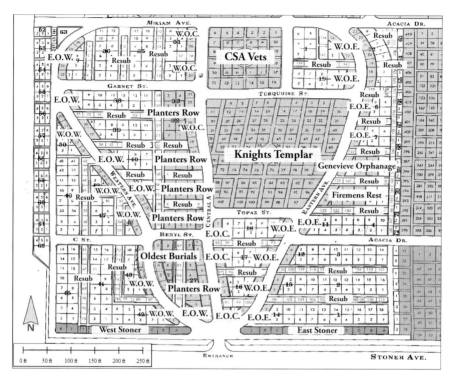

Map of the southwestern portion of Greenwood Cemetery with the main entrance at the bottom and Miriam Avenue at the top. *Cartography by Gary D. Joiner.*

Block 54

Beginning at Garnet Street, turn right on Miriam Avenue. On your left are several monuments from different decades. Walking along the street curb of this section, you see the marker for Dr. Samuel A. Dickson, one of the most popular mayors in Shreveport history.

Block 36

Traveling northeast on Miriam, among the intricately laced sidewalks you find a diamond-shaped cylindrical granite stone that is remarkably constructed. The Vordenbaumen family built the city's main hardware store, located on Milam Street and now familiarly known as the Uneeda Biscuit building. Walking through the interior of this block, you see the unique monument for Lucy Vordenbaumen.

Confederate Veterans' Bivouac

South of Miriam Avenue, after Central Avenue, you see the Confederate Veterans' Bivouac.[35] The square is dominated by a tall column topped with a Confederate soldier standing guard among the first official rests. A flagpole beside the column flies the first national flag of the Confederacy and, below it, the Richard Taylor flag, the emblem of the Army of the Trans-Mississippi, headquartered in Shreveport. The pedestal inscription reads:

> This Stone Is Raised As
> A Tribute of Love and Loyalty
> To His Old Comrades in Arms
> By Peter Youree,
> Capt. Commanding Co. I,
> Slaybacks Regiment,
> Joe Shelby's Brigade,
> Missouri Cavalry.

> "Their Glory Shall Never Die;
> Their Epitaphs
> Are Written in tthe
> Hearts of Mankind;
> And Wherever There Is
> Speech of Noble Deeds,
> Their Names Shall Be
> Held in Remembrance."

> "A Folded Flag,
> A Brilliant Song
> A Deathless Song
> Of Southern Chivalry."

Walking through the interior of this rest, and among the honored dead, you see markers for Andrew Currie, a popular Shreveport mayor; Victor Grosjean, the best-known regional newspaperman of his era and a strong advocate for the Redeemers, those who sought to return to home rule and the end of Reconstruction; William Daniel Townsend and Alexander Worley, two of the last living Confederates; and Reverend Matthew Van Lear (across Oleander Avenue), one of the most beloved ministers of First Presbyterian Church in Shreveport.

Confederate monument. *Image by the author.*

Block 6

On the east side of Eastern Avenue and opposite the Ascension Commandery, Knights Templar Rest, on the right you see a small rest. The Genevieve Orphanage Rest dates to 1899, when the orphanage was created to honor the memory of Genevieve Penick, a little girl who died from choking on her doll's glass eye.[36] The Genevieve Orphanage Rest is the third oldest, only preceded by the Potters' Field and Confederate Veterans' Bivouac.[37]

Block 9

Adjacent to the Genevieve Orphanage Rest on the west are two lots dedicated to the indigent population. Many more would come. The city council minutes book read that a fifty-dollar donation was made for the two lots, listing the purpose as a "Home for the Homeless."[38]

Block 5

South of the Genevieve Orphanage Rest and across a double sidewalk is the Fireman's Rest.[39] The need for this arose due to the death of the city's first professional fireman in the line of duty, in 1899. Michael Roach's ornate cruciform tree stone is in the center.

Block 10

Between the Fireman's Rest and Eastern Avenue is another small rest for a "Home for the Homeless."

Block 11

South of the Fireman's Rest on the north side of Acacia Drive lies a young woman in a "borrowed" curbed plot. Marie Curtis was a locally famous prostitute during the early years of the legal prostitution district. Her obituary was equal to that of a celebrity.

Block 12

South of Acacia Drive and near Eastern Avenue, you see the Ellerbe family tomb. The Ellerbes and the Leonards were related by marriage, and their story is the history of southeastern Caddo Parish, agriculture and journalism. Walking through the interior of this block, you see the beautiful cenotaph for the Ellerbe family. This route brings you back to the main entrance.

TOUR 2. NORTH OF MIRIAM AVENUE AND ALONG OLEANDER AVENUE

The northwestern portion of Greenwood is quite different from the older section. The land falls away to the west and the north. The high ridge is evident as you drive or stroll.

What to See

The design and the master plan for Greenwood's landscape is the brainchild of Jon Emerson, a retired professor from the LSU Robert Reich School of Landscape Architecture.[40] He worked with the City of Shreveport Public Assembly and Recreation (SPAR) department, the Shreveport Garden Study Club and the Friends of Greenwood Cemetery to transform Greenwood into a parklike setting. The implementation is still ongoing, but Emerson worked on the concept for fifteen years, beginning in 2000.[41]

The Pavilion

Beginning at Western Avenue, where it becomes Miriam Avenue, on the left is a modern structure. The roofed open-air venue is known as the Pavilion. It contains a columbarium, a repository for ashes from deceased individuals who did not wish to be buried. The columbarium contains two monoliths containing niches and urn placement, and the Pavilion displays panels describing Greenwood's history.[42]

The Dell

Standing in the Pavilion, gazing north, you see the water feature in the easternmost part of the ravine now called the Dell. The water is held in place by an earthen berm dam built for that purpose. The low area was the home of the pest house, and evidence of some burials was found there. The ground was later consecrated before the pond was built. Many of the hospitalized Confederate Marine Hospital patients as well as tuberculosis patients were interred on the high ground to the north, west of the New Pay Row section.

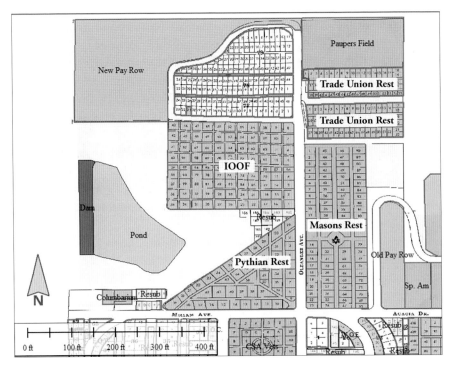

Map of the northwestern portion of Greenwood Cemetery with Miriam Street at the bottom. *Cartography by Gary D. Joiner.*

Pythian Rest

A stroll to the east brings you to a complex triangular section crisscrossed with sidewalks. The Pythian Rest is bordered by Miriam Avenue, Oleander Avenue and the edge of the low area. The local lodge purchased this triangle from the city and surveyed it with specific intentions.[43] The triangle and other geometric figures are significant to the Knights of Pythias. The order's crest is a group of four triangles enclosing an overall triangle. Some of the monuments in this rest contain this symbol with the initials "FCB," standing for Friendship, Charity and Benevolence.[44]

The best-known burial in the Pythian Rest is the grave of a child who donated the first dollar to the construction of the "new" First Methodist Church in Shreveport. Her selfless act was later rewarded with a stained-glass window in her honor at the church at the head of Texas Street. Walking through the interior of this rest, you see the granite monument for Ida Lee Chapman.

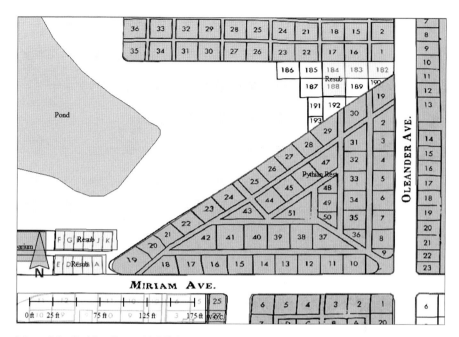

Map of the Pythian Rest with Miriam Avenue at the bottom. Contour lines at two-foot intervals show the sharp drop into the Dell. *Cartography by Gary D. Joiner.*

Masons' Rest

Traveling north on Oleander Avenue, the Pythian Rest is to the left. On the right is the first and oldest of two dedicated Masonic rests.[45] The Masons' Rest contains ninety large plots. The rest consists of four long segments.

Off-center to the south is a large concrete circle with shrubs forming a border on three sides. At the center is a prominent concrete symbol consisting of a compass (divider) and a square with the distinctive *G* at its center. This secretive group openly displays symbols, but it holds its meanings closely. For example, the *G* may stand for God or geometry.[46]

Masons' Rest features many significant monuments. Please take time to walk among them. Through the interior of this rest, you see markers for Dr. James C. Willis, a cofounder of what became the Willis-Knighton Health System. He lies in Lot 27 just east of Oleander Avenue. He was a healthcare pioneer in this region.

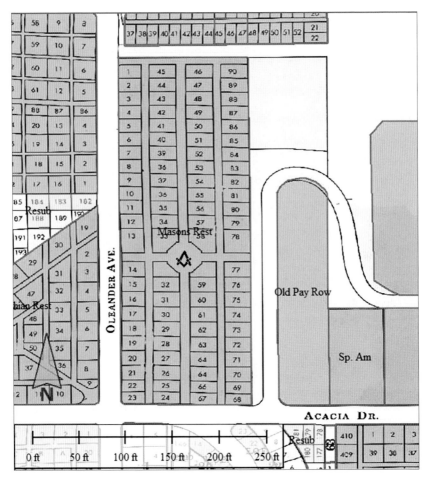

Map of Masons' Rest with Acacia Drive at the bottom. *Cartography by Gary D. Joiner.*

A.C. Steere lies to the east in Lot 27. He was the developer of neighborhoods in Shreveport that made the city's residential landscape what it is today. Steere's pioneering concepts led to the development of South Highlands, Broadmoor and parts of Highland neighborhoods.

The Wheless family cenotaph rises northeast of the Masonic symbol. They were timber barons and civic leaders. This massive granite monolith is easily recognized as one of the symbols of Greenwood.

The Norton family plot lies to the northeast of the Wheless cenotaph. A large black granite curved bench dominates it. The Norton family owns and operates Shreveport's Norton Art Gallery. They are philanthropists of the highest order.

The Masonic symbol in Greenwood Cemetery. *Image by the author.*

Laura May Ferguson lies in a row of graves indistinguishable by boundary between Acacia Loop and Masons' Rest. These are a single row of pay row burials. Adjoining Lot 75 of Masons' Rest is her small vertical tombstone. The child's tragic death is detailed in the iconography on the stone. Most miss this monument. Sitting on top of it, carved with the marble in a single piece, are two baby shoes, one with its sole up and the other facing down as if carelessly cast there and waiting for her to return for them.

Old Pay Row Section

The Old Pay Row section extends across Acacia Loop for a short distance to the Spanish-American War section. It is bordered on three sides by the loop and Acacia Drive. The term "pay row" is spelled interchangeably with "payrow." Greenwood has three pay row sections. "Pay row" is an odd term and was not used in Shreveport before creating this rest. It speaks to the times and hardships in society. Paupers were buried at city expense in the small Home for the Homeless rests. People who could afford family plots owned them. In the broad middle during hard times were the dead of families who could not afford the cost of a typical funeral in a funeral home or church. Greenwood is a municipal cemetery. Therefore, as long as room exists, people are buried in it. Pay rows filled this need. The family paid the sexton to open and close the grave and could, if possible, add a tombstone later.

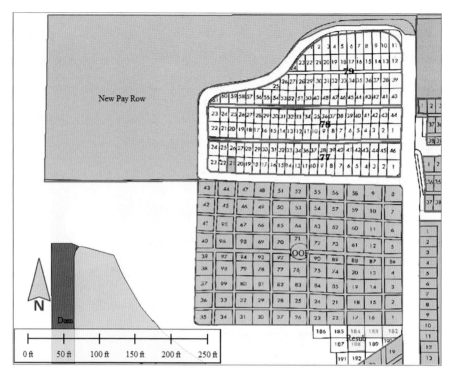

Map of IOOF Rest, the westernmost New Pay Row, the LSU Medical School monument and grave and the third Home for the Homeless Rest, located west of Oleander Avenue. *Cartography by Gary D. Joiner.*

Independent Order of Odd Fellows

Driving north on Oleander Avenue from the Pythian Rest, several rests are on both sides of the street. First, look to the left. The next rest is a large, well-kept rectangle belonging to the Independent Order of Odd Fellows (IOOF). It is easily identified by large, pressed concrete block gate posts and a marble plaque. The marble plaque shows three interlinked chain links with the letters *F*, *L* and *T*. The letters reflect the secret society's motto: "Friendship, Love, and Truth."

The local lodge that purchased this tract in Greenwood was the Neith Lodge, No. 21. It initially requested to purchase Block 27 at the cemetery entrance but was denied on March 16, 1903. The city sold the current rest in 1904.[47] The rest also includes the women's affiliate members, the Daughters of Rebekah, Queen Esther No. 14. The symbolism for the Rebekahs can be stunningly intricate and varied. The symbols are not uniform, but

Left: IOOF entrance. *Image by the author.*

Below: Map of the first trade union rests and the Paupers' or Potters' Field located east of Oleander Avenue. *Cartography by Gary D. Joiner.*

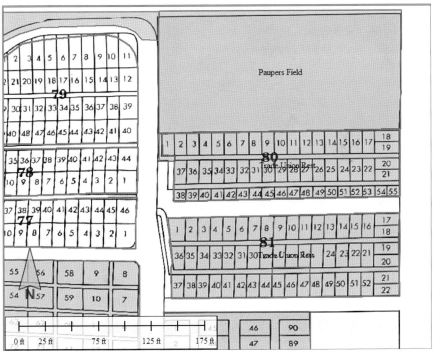

most include a scrolled *D* and *R* and portray a crescent moon motif. It is worthwhile to stroll this section.

Old Trade Union Rests

Oleander Avenue continues north and loops to the west before returning to itself at the northeast corner of the IOOF Rest. To the right, you see two terraced rests. Blocks 80 and 81 are separated by a grassy strip that may be an undeveloped street. Block 81 is divided from the Masons' Rest by another strip, which may have been a designated street. These blocks were the first trade union rests. The only union identified by a monument is the Shreveport Typographical Union No. 155. These workers served local newspapers with stenography (transcription), inking, lithography (printing the paper from metal plates) and other technical skills. By 1942, the union burials had held five members of the ten allotted.[48] Other unions have members here, including several railroad workers. Other graves contain burials of family members of union members.

Eddington Home for the Aged

Lots 45 to 47 of Block 81 were sold to the Eddington Home for the Aged as a separate rest for their clients.[49] This rest dates to 1898 and was the inspiration of two sisters, Dick Files and Rhoda Files Hunter.[50] They created the Home for the Aged, which eventually became the Glen.[51]

The Potters' Field

North of Block 80 and east of Oleander Avenue is a rest that tilts down to the northeast and extends to the north boundary fence of the Greenwood. Few tombstones are visible. This open grassy area is the Paupers' Field or the Potters' Field. Several decades of mowing, sublimation of the soil and perhaps vandalism have removed the slender tombstones for the destitute and at least one villain. Some

Opposite: Pauper marker 765 was found in the rear of the Old Trade Union Rest. *Image by Julianna Horrell.*

Above: Potters' Field view from Oleander Avenue. *Image by the author.*

graves were intentionally not marked so that the curious would not find them. Chief among these was the body of a man named D.P. Napier or Fred Lockhart. He was a serial murderer known locally as the Butterfly Man. After he brutally butchered a local teenage girl, his capture and trial produced a riot, desecration of the then-new Caddo Parish courthouse and nationwide headlines reporting the heinous crime. Local authorities refused to mark his grave, hoping that no one would come to visit him. His unmarked grave can be found by looking to the east at the northern end of Oleander Avenue.

At one time, this grassy field, parts of the old wagon road and the ravine called the Dell featured at least eight hundred thin numbered Georgia marble strips. Some of the graves later received ordinary tombstones, but most did not. Instead, the City of Shreveport paid for two hundred two-foot-long, four-inch-wide, two-inch-thick markers from Hilliard Brothers, stonemasons.[52] Later, two hundred more marble strips were purchased through Robson, Stewart & McGuirk Company.[53] The city purchased hundreds more over the years. As space filled up in the Potters' Field, indigent burials were placed where space could be found, but always out of sight from the rests and formal blocks. None of the indigent stones stand upright today. When found, they are in out-of-the-way places. Shreveport later purchased railroad spikes with numbers stamped into them because they were cheaper than marble. Some of these have been found north of the veterans' lots section and paralleling the wagon road.

LSUMC

A single monument stands at the northern end of Oleander Avenue. The gray granite stone is dedicated to those who donate their bodies to science. Engraved at the top are the letters "LSUMC" (Louisiana State University Medical Center), now the LSU Health Sciences Center. Below this is "Donors to Medical Science," then "MORTUI VIVOS DOCENTI" (The Dead Teach the Living). Once the bodies have yielded all of their information, they are cremated, and the ashes, if not returned to the donor's family, are interred here. Effectively, this is the smallest rest in Greenwood.

Marine Hospital Burials

Following the Oleander Avenue loop to the west, then south, blocks 77 to 79 are on the left. The large sloping area to the right is the New Pay Row section (the first of two). Graves near the street are orderly in placement and in neat rows. The ground slopes to the west and is a grassy area full of unmarked graves. Here are the Confederate dead from the Marine Hospital and many unfortunate tuberculosis victims who died at the pest house.

Driving east on the loop, the IOOF Rest is on the right. Immediately past the curve in Block 77, Lot 21 is another small Home for the Homeless.[54]

Driving east to Oleander Avenue and then south to Acacia Drive ends this portion of the tour.

TOUR 3. MILITARY HEROES, PROUD IMMIGRANTS AND TRAGEDY

This portion of the tour covers the area west of the Old Pay Row Rest and north of Acacia Drive. Again, a stark contrast between the western and eastern halves is evident.

What to See

The extensive veterans' rests lie on both sides of Acacia Loop. You will note that orderly rows of similar tombstones speak to military precision. The origin of these rests began with a request to the Building and Grounds Committee of the Shreveport City Council to define the cost of expanding Greenwood. Unfortunately, the choice lots were taken, and the cemetery soon would run out of room.[55] Because the committee never seemed to act quickly, four years later, they recommended that the city advertise bids for a tract ranging from 20 to 100 acres.[56] Five years after this, the committee announced it would receive offers of not less than 100 acres or not more than 500 acres.[57] The city was authorized to purchase from E.R. Bernstein and J.H. Jordan 67.2 acres known as the Fort Humbug tract.[58] This sale added land to Greenwood Cemetery, but not as much as might have been expected. The southwest corner of this parcel was roughly at the southeast corner of the Old Pay Row Rest and extended roughly eastward along

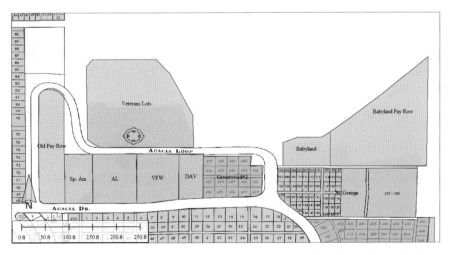

Map of the area north of Acacia Drive and west of the Old Pay Row Rest. *Cartography by Gary D. Joiner.*

Acacia Drive and then due east along the southern line of the St. George Greek Orthodox section. Outside the cemetery, it included the parcel where the Caddo Juvenile Court complex is located today, as well as the Fort Humbug headquarters and armory and the Overton Brooks Veterans Administration Hospital grounds. It left the Stoner Hill neighborhood that borders the cemetery intact. This purchase, plus a later tract added in 1925, became known as Greenwood No. 2.

American Legion and the Veterans of Foreign Wars

Four years after Greenwood opened, the United States fought the short Spanish-American War. Then, America entered the Great War (World War I) in 1917. By 1927, the older veterans of these wars began to die,

The artillery piece central monument in the Veterans of Foreign Wars section. *Image by the author.*

and the city decided to place them in dedicated soldiers' rests, similar to those at Arlington National Cemetery. Accordingly, the Shreveport City Council passed two ordinances on June 14, 1927. The first was a plot dedicated to the American Legion.[59] The second dedicated a rest to the Spanish-American War veterans.[60] Later that year, the Spanish-American War plot was increased by an additional twenty feet.[61] In addition, two more veterans' groups were granted rests in Greenwood. The first was the Veterans of Foreign Wars.[62] The second was the Disabled American Veterans.[63] Later, permission was granted for family members to be buried next to the veterans, provided space was available.

Dominating the north side of the veterans' lots sections is a concrete circle with four plaques in cardinal directions. In the center, raised above this section, is a platform with a flagpole and mounting a 76 mm antiaircraft gun, harkening back to the 204th Coastal Artillery Battery stationed at Fort Humbug.[64]

The military sections do not divide graves into individual plots. Instead, they lie side by side in orderly rows. The founding veterans' groups form the monuments around the flagpole and artillery piece. They are the O.F. Simmons Chapter No. 9, Disabled American Veterans (1937); the J. Milton Edwards Post No. 2238, Veterans of Foreign Wars (1935); the Lowe-McFarlane Post No. 14, American Legion (1935); the Disabled American Veterans of the World War; and the W.H. Mabry Camp, United Spanish-American War Veterans. Walking through the interior of the Spanish-American War section, you see markers for Burch Grabill, a regionally famous photographer; and Willa Norwood, one of only forty army nurses in the Spanish-American War. Buried next to her is her husband, who was allowed there because of her service.

Babyland

Traveling east on Acacia Loop, you see three rests at the curve to the south. Immediately in front is a large ornate iron gate with the word *Babyland* above it. This section is a rest for stillborn babies or infants who died soon after birth. Undoubtedly the saddest area of Greenwood, this space was for children. They are not buried in neat, orderly rows. Instead, the monuments are small, often touching and heartbreaking. Perhaps they are not buried randomly, but appearance evokes this. Some graves have homemade markers. Some were engraved with a finger or a dowel while cement was still wet, while others have petite angels near them. Sadness prevails. Walking through the interior of this rest, you see markers for Charles Dunn and Baby Boy Villarreal.

East of Babyland is a third pay row. This section borders the court complex to the north and the cemetery's eastern boundary.

St. George Greek Cemetery

The well-manicured St. George Greek Cemetery section is south of Babyland and the New Pay Row and at the intersection of Acacia Loop and Acacia Drive. This section was purchased by the Greek fraternal organization AHEPA (the American Hellenic Educational Progressive Association), Local Chapter No. 8, in 1944.[65] In 1922, AHEPA began to promote Hellenism and fought for civil rights and against bigotry and anti-European sentiment fostered by the Ku Klux Klan.[66] This section, built in three parts, has many fine stones. It remains active with room for the future. The stones vary from gleaming white marble to rose, gray and brown granite to stark black granite. The monuments have inscriptions in both Greek and English. Some families have large cenotaphs with smaller ground tablets for individuals. A favorite quest for some is the grave of a local football hero who died in a training accident at the beginning of World War II. His tombstone contains an engraved football. Walking through the interior of this rest, you see a marker for Elefterios "Lefty" Leonardos. This ends the portion of the tour north of Acacia Drive.

The monument in the St. George Greek Cemetery. *Image by the author.*

TOUR 4. GREENWOOD NO. 2

Shreveport grew rapidly with the oil boom of the 1920s, and the mayor and city council decided to expand Greenwood again. The city council authorized the mayor to purchase nineteen acres from S.H. Bolinger, a square immediately east of the original twenty-acre plot of the cemetery.[67] Work commenced quickly, and the new tract became known as Greenwood No. 2.

What to See

The city engineer platted the new portion, but the Masonic Building Company bought a large part of it before much work started. This purchase required a reorganization of the nineteen acres.

Masonic Rest

The Masonic Rest contains 410 lots, roughly uniform in size surrounding a double circle in the center. It is bordered on three sides by Acacia Drive and on the west by the original boundary of Greenwood Cemetery. Gravestones are of various types and sizes, ranging from ground tablets to modern granite single and double stones. Many family members of Masons are buried here. Some of them are extended family members and loved ones. Walking through the interior of Masonic Rest, you see the markers for Samuel Shepherd Caldwell, the beloved three-term mayor who guided Shreveport through most of the Great Depression and World War II; and Martha Segura Nabors.

Lot 418

Driving south from the southern border of St. George Greek Cemetery section on Acacia Drive, Masonic Rest is on the right. A series of remarkable rests is located on the left. Lot 418 of Greenwood No. 2 sits in a roughly rectangular portion that is not in a rest. Located in the curve of Acacia Drive, very close to the pavement, is the grave of the last judicial hangman in Caddo Parish and the last traveling executioner for the State of Louisiana. He executed the Butterfly Man and performed the last legal execution (via the electric chair) in Shreveport. Viewing east from the curb of Acacia Drive is the ground tablet for Bush Kile Jarratt.

Old African American Cemetery

East of the re-subdivided lots is the old African American cemetery. This unofficial rest holds the oldest graves in Greenwood. Most of the burials with markers date to the early to mid-twentieth century. Some newer burials exist. Most, if not all, of the older graves are perhaps pre–Civil War. Their wooden markers have long since disappeared. Nearby Stoner Hill Baptist Church, across Cornwell Avenue, dates to 1914.[68]

The Chinese Section

Close by the southern end of this burial lies another informal rest, that of Shreveport's Chinese community. The most prominent cenotaph here is the magnificent Joe family monument. This highly polished brown granite structure has an interesting quality. If you stand in front of it during the afternoon at different times of the year, the monument seems to float or disappear. The reflective quality of the granite picks up the light of the sun and acts as a mirror.

Modern Trade Unions

The next official rests are located between the Chinese section and Acacia Drive. Again, four trade unions have rests, separated by sidewalks. The boundaries from Acacia Drive were re-subdivided, and some graves there are not associated with the labor union rests. All four trade union rests are aligned perfectly east–west. As you drive along Acacia Drive, watch for four large gravestone-like monuments that announce the rests.

Carpenters' and Joiners' Rest

The northernmost union rest is the United Brotherhood of Carpenters and Joiners of America, Local 764, chartered on November 18, 1901. The

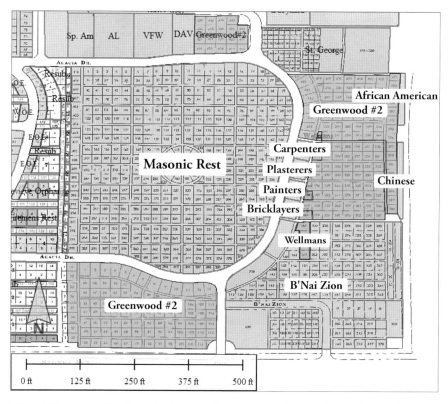

Map of Greenwood No. 2 south of the northern portion of Acacia Drive. *Cartography by Gary D. Joiner.*

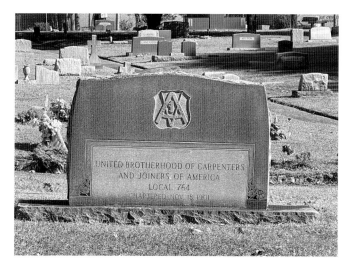

The Carpenters' Rest monument. *Image by the author.*

gray granite stone features a detailed version of the union's crest, adopted in 1884. The artwork contains a rule, a compass and a jack plane inside a shield.[69] The motto in Latin reads *Labor Omnia Vincit*, "Labor Conquers All."

Plasterers' and Cement Finishers' Rest

The next rest is signified by a tall gray granite monument, deeply ornate and heavily incised. The members of the Plasterers and Cement Finishers Local 211 of the Operative Plasterers and Cement Finishers International Association lie in this rest.[70] The granite monument is beautifully finished with ornate flourishes deeply cut into the stone.

Painters' Rest

The third union rest also contains a tall ornate gray granite monument. The crest of the Painters' Rest, Local Union 485 of the Brotherhood of Painters, Decorators and Paperhangers of America, portrays an artist's palette flanked by two rampant lions, above which an eagle is surrounded by stars as in the United States Great Seal.[71] A banner below reads *Labor Omnia Vincit*, "Labor Conquers All."

Bricklayers' Rest

The fourth labor union in this group is the Bricklayers Union Local No. 2 of Louisiana, organized on July 5, 1897. The broad horizontal monument displays two lamps of knowledge above filigreed bases. Today, the union is known as the International Union of Bricklayers and Allied Craftworkers.[72] The crest of the union is, appropriately, a square ruler, level, hammer, mallet, trowel and plumb bob. Unfortunately, visitors often miss one of the most unusual monuments in Greenwood, located in Lot 226 on the southern row of the Bricklayers' Rest. The small stone belongs to the grave of Dessie Alberta Martin. This marble monument is shaped like a house, complete with windows and a Dutch door. A porcelain photograph of Martin is included, and a carved welcome mat lies at its door. Martin's information is on the east or back side of the stone.

Top: The Plasterers' Rest monument. *Image by the author.*

Middle: The Painters' Rest monument. *Image by the author.*

Bottom: The Bricklayers' Rest monument. *Image by the author.*

B'nai Zion

The final rest in Greenwood belongs to the B'nai Zion congregation. The congregation requested—and the city granted—the southeast corner of Greenwood Cemetery.[73] This rest has a dedicated street extending from the main exit and a separate exit gate. Many family plots use borders of hedges or curbs. No standard-sized lots exist. However, subsections are consistent within themselves. The numbering of lots can be baffling if you use only city records. The B'nai Zion Rest contains many beautiful monuments, most conventional, varied in size and color.

A good example is the double monument of Harold and Carolyn Murov. This Shreveport businessman and his loving wife were well known in Shreveport. The couple was active in the community and generous, and both were lifelong learners. They lie in Lot 3F.

A unique, striking double monument, easily seen from Stoner Avenue in Lot 265, belongs to a mother and her son. Nancy and Larry Planchard have two individual monoliths that share a joint base. They differ in height, but both are carved from Indian black granite. Both display myriad finely etched images of mother and son. They commemorate Nancy throughout her adult life and Larry, a surgeon, engineer and master modeler. Most cemetery monuments identify the person buried there, giving their names and dates and perhaps a brief sentiment. Instead, these tell a beautiful, loving story. Both stones describe who they were, what they were like and how much their surviving family and friends loved them. These convey a sense of awe.

Another exotic monument belongs to internationally famed architect William Wiener Sr. The family plot is found in Lot 359. Do not anticipate quickly finding it. A somewhat wild, high hedge borders the lot. Only one entrance and exit exist. Wiener's monument consists of six triangular shafts placed into the ground at an angle. Every viewpoint changes not only the viewer's perspective but also its perceived shape. For example, a Star of David appears only if you look straight into the piece. Wiener's son, William Wiener Jr., a noted architect and sculptor, designed the work. The signature of Wiener graces one of the shafts. Walking through the interior of the B'nai Zion section, you see the monuments for Harold and Carolyn Murov; Larry and Nancy Planchard; and William Wiener.

The tour ends with this rest. The exit gate onto Stoner Avenue is on the left.

LITTLEBERRY CALHOUN ALLEN

32°30"05.1164'N 93°43"53.4763'W
Ascension Commandery Knights Templar Section, Lot 34

L. Calhoun Allen was a two-term mayor (1970–78) who helped guide Shreveport through the turbulent civil rights movement unrest and, as mayor, transformed Shreveport into a stable city that quickly grew. He lies in the Ascension Commandery Knights Templar Section, Lot 34. Examining census records on L. Calhoun Allen can be difficult at best. His grandfather was named Littleberry Calhoun Allen, as was his father, making the mayor the third. People remembered his father but not his grandfather, and the future mayor went along with being called "junior." Further obfuscating the issue, he named his son Littleberry Calhoun Allen III instead of IV.[74]

Littleberry Calhoun Allen.
Northwest Louisiana Archives at LSU-Shreveport.

Mayor Allen had a long service to his country and his city. He was born in Shreveport in 1921. He attended C.E. Byrd High School and Tulane University but graduated from Centenary College, then went to LSU Law School.[75] Allen served in both World War II and the Korean War and retired after thirty-two years of service as a captain in the U.S. Naval Reserve.[76]

He served as a Democrat when politics demanded conservatives in the "Solid South," but Republicans like Presidents Dwight Eisenhower and Gerald Ford were his particular favorites.[77] He was Shreveport's commissioner of public utilities (1962–70), mayor (1970–78), coordinator of plans and development for LSU Medical Center (1979–88) and Council District B councilman from 1990 until his death the following year. He was the commander of the Lowe-McFarlane Post No. 14 and served on the Shreve-area Council of Governments, the Downtown Development Authority and the Shreveport Airport Authority, among many other positions. Shreveport named the new exhibition hall the L. Calhoun Jr. Exhibition Hall following his death.[78]

Allen weathered the turbulent civil rights years unscathed by scandal and, as mayor, firmly dealt with the scandals surrounding his public safety commissioner, George W. D'Artois. The end of the so-called D'Artois era led to the end of overt racism in city government, but the scandals took their toll. Allen tirelessly worked to bring industry to Shreveport and fostered large public works projects, but the scandals overshadowed most of these.[79] He died in the second year of his term on the Shreveport City Council on February 23.

LUCY ELMORE ATKINS

32°30"04.9934'N 93°43"55.8811'W
Ascension Commandery Knights Templar Section, Lot 10

Lucy Elmore

Wife of J.W. Atkins
Born July 12, 1855
Died October 13, 1922
She Was Loyal and True to Her God,
Family and Friends

Maude Lucille
Idolized Daughter Of
J.W. and Lucie Atkins
Born July 10, 1886.
Died October 13, 1910
Her Last Words—
I Love Everybody
I Love God.
I See Heaven. Meet Me There.

The Atkins tomb. *Image by the author.*

The Atkins family tomb commands the northeast corner of the Ascension Commandery Knights Templar section occupying Lot 10. Similar to the nearby tombs of Milton and Ethel Hancock and Dr. T.E. Schumpert, the Atkins tomb is reminiscent of the mausoleum of Cyrus the Great, King of Persia, at Pasargadae, Iran.[80] Unlike the Hancock and Schumpert tombs, there are no outer doors. Instead, the Atkins tomb features three slide-in trays with the occupants' information etched in marble plaques, which seal the inner chambers. The top plaque has no writing. The middle tray contains Lucy Elmore Atkins. The lower tray contains Maude Lucille Atkins. James

Walter Atkins, the family's patriarch, is not in this tomb. He is buried nearby with his second wife, Ethel Colgate Atkins.

James W. Atkins was born in 1860, a native of Neshoba County, Mississippi. He and his brother J.D. moved to Caddo Parish and entered the cotton factor business (buying and selling cotton as middlemen). They were quite successful. In 1889, they handled 3,300 bales valued at $75,000.[81] They also bought land in Red River Parish and grew their own cotton. At the same time, he and another brother opened a large store in Shreveport named J.B. & J.W. Atkins.

James married Lucy (or Lucie) Elmore in 1883. They had four children: an infant daughter who soon died; Maude, who died at age twenty-four and is buried in the Atkins tomb; James, who died at age four; and Herbert, who lived a long life and died at age eighty-one. Lucy died in 1922.[82]

The most striking element of this tomb is the large angel standing over the entrance. It is carved of white marble with intricate feathered wings and gazes down at visitors as they stand before the tomb. The angel holds a bouquet of Madonna (Easter) lilies, a traditional symbol of purity.[83] She has one blossom in her right hand and is poised to drop it, indicating a life that is finished. The tomb was built for Maude, Lucy and J.W. The blank upper marble plaque was to be carved after J.W.'s death. However, following Lucy's death, he married again, and thus the top shelf is empty.

BABYLAND

Babyland. *Image by the author.*

Baby Boy Villarreal
32°30"07.9436'N 93°43"55.8811'W

Babyland is perhaps the saddest section or rest in Greenwood Cemetery. This area contains the graves and monuments dedicated to stillborn children, those who died shortly after birth or only survived a short time. Sometimes the infant was not given a Christian name. For example, the grave of "Baby Boy" Villarreal, born on May 26, 1989, indicates that

Left: Baby Boy Villarreal's grave. *Image by the author.*

Right: Charles Dunn's grave. *Image by the author.*

he lived for less than a day. His ground tablet stone epitaph reads, "Our Angel." This grave remains under care. Located adjacent to the stone are a cement cherub and brightly colored artificial flowers.

Charles Dunn
32°30"07.7517′N 93°43"46.9123′W

Farther to the east is the grave of another child who lived for a day, Charles Dunn. His monument is considered a "folk" memorial. It is composed of concrete poured and molded into a cross. Painted brown, the inscription reads, "AUG 1 1965, CHARLES DUNN, AUG 1 1965," in yellow/orange paint. At the foot of the cross is a rectangular concrete stone. Before it dried, someone—perhaps a parent—wrote in cursive, "Charles Dunn, Forever in Our Hearts, 8-1-65, 8-1-65." These stones have not deteriorated. Most of the graves of children buried here receive attention, regardless of when they were buried.

The image shown here faces east. Charles Dunn's grave is near the top center. Notice on the upper right are two sets of cherubs. They ring an unmarked, unknown grave of a child. The cherubs, made of concrete, are carefully arranged. Someone still cares. A primary characteristic of Babyland is that the children lie in apparent random rows. The original survey plat of the cemetery indicates no organization or plots.

NEWTON CRAIN BLANCHARD

32°30"05.0618'N 93°43"54.4383'W
Ascension Commandery Knights Templar Section, Lot 5

Newton Crain Blanchard
January 25, 1849
June 22, 1922

———

Representative in Congress
United States Senator
Judge Supreme Court
Governor of Louisiana
President Constitution Convention 1913

———

Grant Him Eternal Rest, O Lord,
And May Light Perpetual Shine Upon Him

Governor Newton Crain Blanchard's tomb is easily found in the Ascension Commandery Knights Templar section in Lot 5. It is located at the foot of Oleander Avenue, south of its intersection with Turquoise Street. A large granite Greco-Roman Revival column marks the grave. Atop the structure is a granite urn. At the foot, on a low pedestal, is an amphora-like vase. The graves of Governor Blanchard and his wife, Mary Emily Barret Blanchard, rest under concrete barrel vaults.

New Crain Blanchard's grave site. *Image by the author.*

Newton Crain Blanchard had a spectacular career in local, state and national politics. He served northwest Louisiana as a congressman; and the state of Louisiana as a U.S. senator, a member of the Louisiana Supreme Court, governor and president of the Louisiana Constitution Convention in 1913. Locally, his almost entirely unsung role was to end lynching as a common practice and demand complete jurisprudence for all accused felons.

The *Biographical Dictionary of the United States Congress* lists Blanchard's accomplishments in the legislative branch:

BLANCHARD, Newton Crain, a Representative and a Senator from Louisiana; born in Rapides Parish, La., January 29, 1849; completed academic studies; studied law in Alexandria, La., in 1868 and graduated from the law department of the University of Louisiana in 1870; admitted to the bar and commenced practice in Shreveport, La., in 1871; delegate to the State constitutional convention in 1879; elected as a Democrat to the Forty-seventh and to the six succeeding Congresses and served from March 4, 1881, until his resignation, effective March 12, 1894; chairman, Committee on Rivers and Harbors (Fiftieth, Fifty-second and Fifty-third Congresses); appointed and subsequently elected as a Democrat to the United States Senate to fill the vacancy caused by the resignation of Edward D. White and served from March 12, 1894, to March 3, 1897; was not a candidate for reelection; chairman, Committee on Improvement of the Mississippi River and its Tributaries (Fifty-third Congress); elected associate justice of the supreme court of Louisiana and served from 1897 to 1903, when he resigned; Governor of Louisiana 1904–1908; resumed the practice of law in Shreveport, La.; member of the State constitutional convention in 1913 and served as president; died in Shreveport, La., June 22, 1922.[84]

The National Governors Association website includes his accomplishments in his years as governor:

NEWTON C. BLANCHARD was born in Rapides Parish, Louisiana on January 29, 1849. His education was attained at Louisiana State Seminary of Learning, and at Tulane University, where he earned a law degree in 1870. Blanchard entered politics in 1876, serving as chairman of the Caddo Parish Democratic Committee. He served as a delegate to the 1879 Louisiana Constitutional Convention, and was a member of the U.S. House of Representatives from 1881 to 1894. He was appointed and then elected to the U.S. Senate, serving from 1893 to 1897. He also served as an associate justice of the Louisiana Supreme Court from 1897 to 1903. Blanchard won the 1904 Democratic gubernatorial nomination, was elected governor, and was sworn into office on May 10, 1904. During his tenure, several appointed positions were made into elective offices, public educational programs were advanced, and a state board of forestry was established, as well as a state reform school. Also, a board of charities and corrections was formed, and the Democratic Party primary was initiated. As his term neared an end, he attended the first Conference of Governors in 1908, where he was chosen to head the resolutions committee. After completing his term, Blanchard continued to stay active in public service. In 1913, he served as president of the Louisiana Constitutional Convention, and was a delegate to several Democratic National Conventions. Governor Newton C. Blanchard passed away on June 22, 1922.[85]

Mary Emily Barrett Blanchard was an accomplished woman in addition to being the wife of a successful politician and jurist. She was born in Nacogdoches, Texas, in April 1856, the daughter of Captain William Barret. On her mother's side, she was related to Thomas Rusk, the vice president of the Republic of Texas. He served with General Sam Houston at the Battle of San Jacinto.[86] According to a source who knew her well, "Mrs. Blanchard is of medium height and good figure, with a creamy complexion, rippling dark hair, and dark brown eyes; speaks French well and sings sweetly; is warm-hearted and sympathetic; enjoys society and helps others to have a good time wherever she is."[87]

This couple, who gave so much to Louisiana, is honored in many ways, but today's public may view them as only an asterisk in a political commentary.

WILLIAM ERNEST BLAND

32°30″03.2892′N 93°43″58.0811′W
Block 49, Lot 1

W.E. Bland
Born
December 6. 1863
Died
Oct 16. 1899

Erected by W of W

Most tombstones or monuments tell visitors the bare minimum about the person buried. However, with some additional research, the visitor can discover much more. This monument is located in Block 49, Lot 1, west of Western Avenue. William Ernest Bland was born in Jasper, Jasper County, Texas, on December 6, 1863, and died in Shreveport on October 16, 1899, at the age of thirty-five.[88] The monuments near his grave are of his parents and his wife. Three of his children are buried in Greenwood, as are his siblings.

Visitors are drawn to this monument by its shape, symbols and the sheer intricacy of the artwork. This work is a superb example of a Woodmen of the World tree stone. The Woodmen of the World (WOW) still exist. They began in Omaha, Nebraska, in 1890 and quickly spread from coast to

William Ernest Bland's tree stone. *Image by the author.*

coast. Oddly, it was an insurance company that morphed into a semi-secret fraternal order. The insurance company membership was risk averse. WOW excluded many professions from joining. Some railroad workers, bartenders and many others were not candidates.[89] The Woodmen relaxed many of their rules, and particularly in the South, many members were involved in the lumbering industry. The organization is now the Woodmen of the World Life Insurance Society.[90] One of the primary selling points of the Woodmen was the promise that "no Woodman shall rest in an unmarked grave."[91] They keep that promise to this day, although the ornateness and size have diminished over the years due to cost and societal changes. Greenwood has several excellent examples of WOW monuments. Not all are tree stones. Near Bland's monument are twin spheres or orbs of a husband and wife. Simpler tree trunk designs are found in many rests.

Bland's monument was erected by the Woodmen only nine years after the company's founding. It is constructed of marble and is not a factory piece. Although the company often copied the concept, many details are personalized. The base consists of tiered segments to resemble cut and stacked logs. The ends of the logs have tree growth rings that add up to the deceased's age. The upper tier of the base, facing east, consists of logs and a spectacular anchor and chain. Master stonemasons often used the anchor on Victorian tombstones identifying the virtue of Hope.[92] Over this is draped a tasseled tapestry with Bland's information.

Anchored into this base is a heavily stylized Roman cross in the form of a tree stump. Knots and closely cut limb bases adorn the cross, and the two cross arms and the top are perfectly cut to show where the limbs were harvested. The heart of the wood is perfectly smooth, but the bark is peeling back to reveal the wood. The peeled bark is uneven and appears to be roughly torn. The symbology is the shedding of mortal life to reveal perfection. The crux of the stump contains one of several early WOW insignias. It has a complicated structure. At the center is a log with a mallet resting over it. A dove in flight soars above the log. Below this, forming almost a circle on the sides of the log and dove, is a banner that reads, "DUM TACET CLAMAT" (Though Silent, He Speaks). A thin ring encloses this motif. Extending around the top half of the emblem is another curved piece that reads "WOODMEN OF THE WORLD."

This monument is exceptionally delicate. It is prone to lichen growth. Visitors should never attempt to clean or rub anything against it, especially over the WOW insignia.

SAMUEL SHEPHERD CALDWELL

32°30"04.8800'N 93°43"48.6893'W
Masonic Rest, Lot 150

Samuel Shepherd Caldwell. *Northwest Louisiana Archives, LSU-Shreveport.*

Lying in the Masonic Rest in Lot 150 is the man who led Shreveport through the worst of the Great Depression and throughout World War II. Samuel Shepherd Caldwell was a three-term mayor from 1934 through 1946. He was the longest-serving mayor before Clyde Fant. Caldwell was a native of Mooringsport in northern Caddo Parish, born in November 1892.

When his third term ended, Caldwell became the executive vice president of the Louisiana-Arkansas Division of Mid-Continent Oil and Gas Association.[93] He ran a grassroots campaign for governor and did not win. Still, his pledges to the public remained the same: education assistance for returning soldiers and sailors, protecting the "rights of all people," "a real home rule policy, and an absolutely square deal for both labor and capital."[94]

Caldwell became ill in April 1953 due to a lung ailment that would not heal. His local doctors sent him to the Mayo Clinic in Rochester, Minnesota. The physicians there operated. He recuperated at a "local sanitarium," but his condition worsened, and he died.[95]

A eulogy ran as an editorial in the *Shreveport Times* and covered most of a double-wide column.[96] Caldwell—"Sam" to all who knew him—was the perfect man in bad times. During the Great Depression, local funds were largely nonexistent to run the city, and federal funds for major projects were long in coming. Despite these significant obstacles, he focused on people's needs first and foremost. Public healthcare was in tatters. He revitalized the first local health unit in cooperation with the longtime coroner, Dr. Willis Butler. The efficient model used in Shreveport became nationally recognized by the federal public health services, encompassing prenatal, maternity, postnatal and dental clinics.[97] Shreveport's relatively sizeable public park system had "exactly one park bench, and no nothing more, as park equipment."[98] During Caldwell's third term in World War II, he created what would later become SPAR, Shreveport Parks and Recreation, which is today's Shreveport Public Assembly and Recreation. He added Ford Park on Cross Lake and Querbes Park and built the USO building in Princess Park, much later destroyed by fire. Service members traveling east or west and stopped over in Shreveport had a place to rest, eat and be entertained, making Shreveport a model for other cities. The *Shreveport Times* summed up how people viewed Sam Caldwell:

> *Personal forthrightness and frankness of utterances even when it was politically expedient to speak, plus insistence that political government simply is a public business that has to be operated on the same basis as private business, were outstanding traits of Sam Caldwell—probably the outstanding traits in his character. He was as honest as the day was long, a gentleman in every way.*[99]

Before his first term as mayor, northern Caddo Parish elected Caldwell to the Caddo Parish Policy Jury. During his tenure as mayor of Shreveport, Caldwell served as the Louisiana vice president of the U.S. Conference of Mayors and was chairman of the Louisiana Municipal Association.[100]

IDA LEE CHAPMAN

32°30"07.5737'N 93°43"55.5786'W
Pythian Rest, Lot 45

Ida Lee
Daughter of
H.A. and M.E. Chapman
November 30 1900–May 7 1911
A Little Child Shall Lead Them
Was True in Her Beautiful Life
She Was a Faithful Christian
And a Devoted Member of the
Methodist Church
Chapman

The Pythian Rest is located north of Miriam Avenue and anchored on Oleander Avenue. This rest is in the shape of a triangle with complex geometric sidewalks befitting the custom of the Knights of Pythias. Lot 45 contains the grave and tombstone of Ida Lee Chapman. She died at age ten but was well known in Shreveport. Ida was the daughter of Hiram Alexander Chapman and Mary E. Ida Chapman. Her father, who worked at Lee Hardware, is buried near her in Pythian Rest, and her mother is buried nearby in the Independent Order of Oddfellows section. Ida was mentioned prominently in society column articles during her brief life. She was loving

Ida Lee Chapman's tombstone.
Image by the author.

and devoted to her family, friends and First Methodist Church in Shreveport.[101] The *Shreveport Journal* ran a column following Ida's death that displayed the outpouring of grief.[102] Ida's father attended the annual Methodist Conference in December 1911, and the *Shreveport Times* reported receiving condolences from the attendees. The paper stated, "Everyone knew of the beautiful memorial to be erected to her memory [the stained-glass window] and took occasion to offer that balm to her father's heart."[103]

First Methodist raised funds to build its current magnificent church at Texas and Common Streets, and Ida was the first person to contribute. Her donation was a silver dollar, quite a sum for a ten-year-old child in 1911. Although this was not known for almost sixty years, the senior minister, Reverend G.E. Cameron, did not spend this silver dollar.

She did not see the church completed, but her act of kindness and premature death is reflected today. One of the magnificent stained-glass windows in the church contains her likeness. The church named the building fund in her memory.[104] In addition to the stained-glass window in her memory, the Junior Epworth League supported a scholarship in Suchow, China, selling candy to raise funds.[105]

In April 1970, Dr. D.L. Dykes Jr., the senior minister at First Methodist Church, opened the cornerstone of First Methodist Church in front of his congregation. He removed a sealed metal box that contained several artifacts when the cornerstone was laid on April 27, 1913. Inside was a pressed rose and a handwritten message from then pastor G.W. Cameron and his wife, Stella Gibson Cameron. However, most attention was focused on Ida Lee's 1899 silver dollar, the first donation toward the new sanctuary.[106]

ANDREW W. CURRIE

32°30″07.5737′N 93°43″55.5786′W
Confederate Veterans' Bivouac, Lot 3

PVT
Andrew W Currie
Capt. Nutt's
Co La Cav
CSA
Mar 4, 1843
Feb 8, 1918

Located in Lot 3 of the Confederate Veterans' Bivouac and immediately south of Mirium Avenue is the grave of a man who displayed the epitome of civic service.[107] Andrew Currie was born in Ibricken, County Clare, Ireland, in 1843. He sailed across the Atlantic at six, landing in Boston with two of his brothers, and ten years later, he made Shreveport his home for more than fifty years.[108] He joined the Confederate army when the Civil War began and entered as a private in Company A, Caddo Rifles, First Louisiana Volunteer Infantry Regiment.[109] Currie was captured at Arkansas Post and remained a prisoner at a prisoner of war camp in Springfield, Illinois.[110] He was paroled, returned to service and captured at Rome, Georgia, a second time, then found himself at Camp Morton, another POW camp near Indianapolis, Indiana.[111] He was paroled after the war and returned to Shreveport, where he became a popular and progressive member of society. He was a proud member of General Leroy Stafford Camp No. 3 of the United Confederate Veterans. In almost everything he attempted, Currie had something of a golden touch. For example, he held some political offices simultaneously.

According to Findagrave.com, Andrew Currie served as:

Deputy Sheriff, Caddo Parish
Constable, Caddo Parish
Shreveport City Fire Chief, 1881
Mayor of Shreveport, 1878–90
Louisiana State Senator, 1892–96
Postmaster, 1896–1901
Shreveport City Council Member, 1900–10
Owner and Operator of the *Shreveport Times*[112]

According to the *Shreveport Times* news story of his death:

> *Returning to Shreveport,* [Currie] *went into business and also made the start of a long and honorable career in politics, during which he held almost every position in the gift of the voters. He was a police juror, state senator from Caddo Parish from 1892 to 1896, mayor of the city from 1878 to 1890, a member of the City Council for seven years after 1890, and postmaster under President Cleveland.*
>
> *It was while he was mayor that the Red river was bridged, and the V.S. & P.* [Vicksburg, Shreveport and Pacific] *brought to the city, largely through his efforts. The Kansas City Southern also was brought through Shreveport about this time.*
>
> [Currie] *entered into the insurance business in 1876 and continued in it until early in the present century.…He was an owner of the* Shreveport Times *in the early nineties. He early realized the possible growth and development of the city, and invested heavily in real estate.…He opened up the West Shreveport*[113] *section for development.*
>
> *Mr. Currie was a member of Holy Trinity Catholic Church, and donated the church cemetery. He is also the donor of children's playgrounds in West Shreveport. With regard to his private benefactions, only those whom he helped can tell of its extent.*[114]

The *Shreveport Journal*, although in a shorter article, was no less complimentary. It ended with, "So, the chronicle of achievement Mr. Currie

Left: Andrew Currie. *From McClure and Howe,* History of Shreveport and Shreveport Builders, *p. 257.*

Right: Andrew Currie's tombstone. *Image by the author.*

created will last, though future generations may recall little or nothing of his identity. By his fruits history will judge him; and they are rich indeed.

"Andrew Currie was a loyal citizen, a faithful public servant and a good man. Requiescat en pace."[115]

Currie had been ill for three weeks before his death. According to the *Shreveport Times*, he died of broncho-grippe. Today, we know this was an early case of what would become known as the "Great Influenza."

This man who did so much for Shreveport does not lie under a vast, magnificent monument. Instead, he rests with his brothers under arms with a simple Civil War Confederate stone at his request.

MARIE CURTIS

32°30″07.5737′N 93°43″55.5786′W
Block 11, Lot 4

Marie Curtis
Born 1885
Died
June 26, 1907

Marie Curtis's tombstone. *Image by the author.*

Near the southern intersection of Eastern Avenue and Acacia Drive is a concrete bordered lot labeled "Sanders." It holds a single grave and the stone, broken into three pieces, still with wording legible. The grave contains the remains of Marie Curtis, age twenty-one. No photos exist of her, but Shreveport knew her well. She died during the legal red-light period, which began in 1903 and lasted until 1907. She was a prostitute of some renown. The sexton's records state that she died of "syphilis of the brain."[116] Marie's obituary ran as a news story in the Sunday edition of the *Shreveport Times*. She died on June 26, and her funeral was on Saturday, June 29. The uncredited story ran almost one thousand words:

Touch of Nature

Pitiful Scenes Surround the Passing Away of Worldly Unfortunate

Beautiful Wayward Woman

Far From Home and Loved Ones, Draining Sorrow's Cup to the Bitter Dregs, Marie Curtis Found Final Resting Place in City of Dead with Angry Elements in Uproar.

Another mound was erected in the Silent city of the dead during the past week, and Mother Earth was the Richer in claiming the body of one more unfortunate.

When the lengthening shadows of even fell across the fresh made mound, they found a rare collection of the choicest of flowers, tokens of friendly feeling from a host of the friends of this unfortunate girl, just turning her twenty-first birthday, the age when the majority of young women are entering upon happy careers. In the coming of the eventide, a minister of the Gospel, one of God's chosen men, consigned the mortal remains of this sin-ridden girl to the bosom of Mother Earth, and the great busy world moved on in its mad race, unmindful of the promising career that had been terminated in a whirl of gay and thoughtless dissipation, or of the sinister form of the One Man responsible that loomed in the murky background.

Marie Curie was the name by which she was known. Five short years ago she came to Shreveport from St. Louis. Her mother, reputed to be an estimable woman, now resides at Cairo, Ill., and is said to be the proprietor of a respectable place of public amusement—a moving picture show. When she was telegraphed the news of her wayward daughter's death, her finances were low, but she gathered together her mite and started eighty dollars toward Shreveport for a simple funeral, asking that the body be embalmed that she might, in some brighter, future day, ship it back to the little plot that holds other loved ones who have passed before.

Eighty dollars represented this lonely woman's best contribution to the burial of her daughter in a far off land. Those former associates of the dead woman, who led a short life and a merry one, promptly raised several hundred of dollars, and stopped the coming of the pitiful eighty dollars that had been started on their way.

Wedded and Parted

Some years before, according to the story told by the friends of this lonely and unfortunate girl, she was happily wed. The tide of life ran roughly, however, misfortune overtook their household, and the man who swore to love honor and protect her forgot those Altar vows. Abundantly supplied with nature's rarest gifts of beauty and talent, thrown helpless upon the world, the craven creature that lurks in man's form quickly sought his prey. Her after-story is a repetition of that pitiful experience of but too many women.

Five years ago she came to Shreveport, so it is said, a queen among women, endowed with rare beauty and stateliness. At once she became a reigning queen within the walls of those structures too commonly believed to be gilded palaces of sin, but which are, in reality, often bare and barren, and where conscience, once unburdened with wine or drug, wracks the unfortunate victim to the verge of distraction that frequently results in the shorter route of suicide.

Queen of Tenderloin

Gay, thoughtless and careless, this specimen of womanly physical beauty soon numbered her friends by the hundreds. She became what is termed a "good fellow," and the pace she set was just a little swifter than even the swiftest had ever before attempted to go. Her pace was, verily, the pace that kills. Five years it took to kill her, five years of forgetfulness—unmixed pain, sorrow and disappointment, but they ended with a siege of weeks in the hospital and then her outraged nature was compelled to abdicate.

The night before the internment, when the cold and lifeless clay rested in the parlors of a downtown undertaking establishment, three friends of former days, who have endeavored to maintain the same killing pace, or who pitied her for the early misfortune of her misspent life, sent flowers of the highest perfection of the florist's creation. Every design was immaculate in preparation and manner of treatment, their undefiled purity contrasting strangely with the visible marks of dissipation that even the kindly hands of Death were unable to obliterate.

Demons at War

Eight carriages followed the hearse to Greenwood cemetery, and scions of prominent families sorrowfully witnessed the last kindly act. As the minister pronounced the words of the beautiful burial ritual, and the new-made mound assumed its familiar proportions, only to be buried deep beneath the tokens of remembrance that spread in every direction from the last silent home of the little woman, the angry elements came hurtling from the northeast. To the impressionable who stood around the little grave, the shrieking of the wind took unto itself the semblance of the enraged cry of a defeated demon, and in one's imaginative eye the minions of Satan could be pictured in their wrath as the Angel of Love came to the repentant little woman and bore her soul on High. Over in the Half World, where, perhaps, it is surprising to know that the lines of social demarcation are even more tightly drawn than in the great world outside, a pall of sorrow hung over the associates of the lone little occupant of that lonely grave in beautiful Greenwood cemetery, and the popping of the champagne corks failed to arouse the usual gay and thoughtless laughter. Up in that desolate Illinois home a letter has been received, perhaps today, that sang only the virtues of the little unfortunate, and an aged mother is spared the anguish that must have followed a realization that her own little daughter had played the part of a thoroughbred in the swiftest race that man may know.[117]

Marie Curtis's succession was opened in the First District Court in Shreveport after her death. F.A. Leonard, the clerk of court, was appointed administrator. Her estate consisted of the value of her property, valued at $300.[118] Her worldly goods were auctioned to the highest bidder at noon in front of the Caddo Parish Courthouse on July 31, 1907.[119]

REVEREND WILLIAM TUCKER
DICKINSON DALZELL

32°30"04.3186'N 93°43"55.1365'W
Knights Templar Ascension Commandery Section, Lot 54

W.T. Dickinson
Dalzell, D.D.
June 7, 1827.
February 4, 1899.
Rector St. Mark's
Episcopal Church
1866–1899

One of the great heroes of nineteenth-century Shreveport, Reverend William Tucker Dickinson Dalzell, lies buried in Lot 54 of the Knights Templar Ascension Commandery Section.[120] Reverend Dalzell was born on the Caribbean island of St. Vincent in 1827.[121] Many authorities believed that he contracted a mild case of yellow fever there, and it led to his immunity to that scourge. However, he was not afraid of it and worked to relieve suffering due to "Yellow Jack," as it was called.

The young Dalzell was educated in England, graduating from Oxford University with degrees in medicine and the ministry. He was ordained in the Church of England. The Reverend Dr. Dalzell sailed across the Atlantic for Kingston, Jamaica. His father was a sugar plantation owner in St. Vincent, and the post suited him well. He then moved to Philadelphia, Pennsylvania,

Reverend W.T.D. Dalzell's cross. *Image by the author.*

before moving to the South. Dalzell was sent to Norfolk, Virginia, in 1854 to help with an outbreak of yellow fever. He was appointed deacon and rector of Trinity Episcopal Church in Columbus, Georgia, and served there in 1854–55. He was appointed to the Diocese of Texas in 1859. When the Civil War began, he served as a chaplain in a Texas regiment. Dalzell was

Reverend W.T.D. Dalzell. *From McClure and Howe,* History of Shreveport and Shreveport Builders, *p. 256.*

appointed rector of the Church of Houston and raised money for their first organ. He married Felicity Estelle Logan in New Orleans immediately after the war and moved to Shreveport in 1866 to serve as rector at St. Mark's Episcopal Church.

Shreveport saw one of the most significant yellow fever outbreaks in American history in 1873. Reverend Dalzell might have been the first person to recognize it for the plague. Shreveport's population was about fourteen thousand, and ten thousand fled. Of the remaining four thousand people, three-quarters would contract the disease, and one thousand would perish. The local leaders tried to deny that it was Yellow Jack, but with deaths rising, they listened to Dr. Dalzell, local priests and the surviving physicians. Dalzell was a member of the Howard Association, which aided victims and municipalities fighting the disease. He was the only Protestant minister in Shreveport to remain at his post.[122]

An even more significant outbreak struck Memphis and New Orleans in 1878. Dalzell moved to Memphis to help in the struggle there. When the disease ebbed that winter, he moved his family back to Shreveport and resumed his duties at St. Mark's. Dalzell built a home at 758 Austin Place, from which he could see the ever-present reminder of the mass grave containing over eight hundred dead in the fever mound at Oakland Cemetery. Dr. Dalzell was a renaissance man who was an expert in Masonic law and served Caddo Parish's citizens as school board president for eight years. He was married three times. He died on February 4, 1899. He received a Masonic funeral with full rites conducted by the Caddo Lodge 179, F. and A.M., serving as worshipful master.

Dr. Dalzell's monument is a relatively small cross overpowered by nearby monuments. Yet, like the man it memorializes, the cross defines him for eternity.

JEAN DESPUJOLS

32°30"04.3186'N 93°43"55.1365'W
Re-subdivision Lot 150, adjacent to Block 40

Jean Despujols
Ne   *Mort*
Le 19 Mars 1886   Le 26 Janvier 1965
Prix E La Ville
Medaille D'or De Parish
Premier Grand Prix de Rome de Peinture
Prix De L'Indochine
Croix de Guerre, avec Six Citations
Medaille Militaire
Legion D'Honneur

Jean Despujols, a well-known French artist and hero of World War I, lies in Lot 150 in a re-subdivision of Greenwood. He is in the same block as Pioneers' Rest, roughly equidistant between Western Avenue, Central Avenue and Beryl Street. He was born in Salles, Department de la Gironde, Aquitaine, France, in March 1886 and died in Shreveport in January 1965 at age seventy-eight.[123]

Rarely do the works of an artist of great stature hang in a single venue. Jean Despujols is one of them with his art on display at the Meadows Museum of Art on the campus of Centenary College in Shreveport. Most of the artwork

Right: Jean
Despujols. *Northwest
Louisiana Archives at
LSU-Shreveport.*

Below: Detail of
Jean Despujols's
tombstone. *Image by
the author.*

covers his time in French Indochina, Vietnam, Cambodia and Laos prior to World War II. Despujols fled France before the Nazis invaded and came to Shreveport, where he resided near the Centenary College campus. He was internationally known and became a local celebrity, painting many fine portraits of local citizens.

His granite tombstone faces west, and the inscriptions are in French. Below his name and birth and death dates are seven outstanding accomplishments. The first four are for his artistic honors. The others speak eloquently of his courage. Despujols was awarded during World War I the Croix de Guerre (Cross of War), with six citations; the Military Medal (for service); and the Legion of Honor.

DR. SAMUEL AUGUSTUS DICKSON

32°30"05.5601'N 93°43"59.2472'W
Block 54, Lot 1

Dickson

Dr. Samuel Augustus   Bula Dillngham

Mar. 18, 1862–June 2, 1916   July 14, 1872–Dec. 21, 1964

The tombstone of Dr. Samuel Augustus Dickson and his wife, Bula, is located in Block 54, Lot 1. Dr. Dickson was a two-term mayor of Shreveport and one of the most popular and well-respected figures in the history of Shreveport. He had no trace of bigotry and treated every citizen of Shreveport as equals.[124] Mayor Dickson died suddenly in St. Louis, Missouri, while en route to New York City on public business. The public outpouring of grief has never been equaled or surpassed.

As the *Shreveport Journal* reported, Dr. Dickson's body was brought to Shreveport by the Kansas City Southern Railroad to Union Station, where family and friends met it, along with Elks Lodge members. It was taken to city hall and later moved by the Kansas City Southern Railroad to Union Station. Thousands of men and women, Black and white with no segregated lines, came to pay homage to Dr. Dickson. The body lay in state for four hours in the lobby on a catafalque from noon until 4:00 p.m. City hall was then closed to all but family members and friends. The pallbearers moved the body to a private reception room, where the funeral service was conducted by Dr. Jasper Smith, senior pastor of First Presbyterian Church. Following

Dr. Samuel Augustus Dickson's tombstone. *Image by the author.*

the service, the procession, reported to be in the hundreds, made its way to Greenwood Cemetery, where Dr. Dickson's favorite hymn, "Nearer My God to Thee," was sung by a quartet from the Elks Club. The flowers alone filled three full wagons.[125] The *Shreveport Journal*'s coverage covered all of page twelve, except for advertisements.

The *Shreveport Times*, in the June 22, 1916 issue, posted legal notices. Dr. Dickson died between two city council meetings, and the council passed an unprecedented resolution:

> *The Commissioners as a Committee of the Whole, appointed to draft RESOLUTIONS relative to the death of Mayor S.A. Dickson, made the following report:*
>
> *"On June 2, Anno Domini 1916, the Grim Reaper, seeking, as ever, a shining light, was attracted by the lustre shed by our beloved Mayor, Samuel Augustus Dickson, and summoned him into the presence of the Most High, thereby depriving us of a loyal friend, depriving this family of a loving husband and father, and the City of Shreveport and its citizens of an Executive distinguished even among the great.*
>
> *"Whereas, it has pleased the Almighty God, in His wisdom, to take from our midst and away from our councils Doctor Samuel Augustus Dickson; and,*
>
> *"Whereas, we bow in reverence to the judgments of the Divine power which called our chief away from those of this earth who loved and honored*

him most even while our souls are oppressed with sorrow the most keen sense of personal and official loss; therefore,

"Be it Resolved, By the City Council of Shreveport, Louisiana, in legal and regular session convened: That we hereby express our sincere regret and our most profound sorrow at the death of Doctor Samuel Augustus Dickson, Mayor of Shreveport, that we express our high appreciation of those qualities of manhood which he possessed in such marked degree as to make him stand out with distinction among his fellows, that we will ever regret the passing of our beloved chief.

"Be it further Resolved that, etc.: That we hereby extend our most sincere sympathy and condolences to Mrs. Dickson and the children and family of Dr. Dickson that these resolutions be spread upon the minutes of the Council, and that copies hereof be sent to Doctor Dickson's wife and family."[126]

JOHN HENRY EASTHAM

32°30″03.7877′N 93°43″56.2219′W
Re-subdivision of Greenwood Cemetery Lot 16, between Block 31 and Central Avenue

Eastham
John Henry   *Ellen Mayo*
Sept. 23, 1863   Mar. 9, 1870
Nov. 11, 1938   Aug. 24, 1938

Located in Lot 16 of the re-subdivision of Greenwood between Block 31 and Central Avenue is the grave of Mayor John Henry Eastham. Unfortunately, his tombstone is a flat ground tablet and can be very difficult to locate. He was born in Mansfield, Louisiana, in September 1861 and died in Shreveport in November 1938 at age seventy-seven.[127]

Eastham was well known as an entrepreneur before entering politics. He partnered with Edward Henry Vordenbaumen to create Vordenbaumen and Eastman's hardware business. They excelled in this endeavor and outgrew two buildings before building the tallest building in Shreveport at the time. It still exists after going through many iterations. The building, located at 712 Milam Street, still bears its name, Eastman and Vordenbaumen, on an upper floor and later became for decades Marcus Furniture. It is now under renovation for commercial and residential use. It is best known for its western wall. Although few people will remember Vordenbaumen and

John Henry Eastham's ground tablet. *Image by the author.*

Eastman or Marcus Furniture, many who visit downtown Shreveport know "Uneeda Biscuit." The art on the wall was part of a national advertising campaign by the National Biscuit Company, better known as NABISCO.[128]

Not many politicians leave the office as Eastham did, with the nickname of "Honest John." He guided Shreveport from 1910 to 1914 and was the first mayor under the city commission form of government, which lasted until 1978.[129] He was a Progressive in the mold of Theodore Roosevelt. He believed in the public good, first and always. Shreveport found itself plagued by foul drinking water. He secured funds from the city commission to purchase the swamplands that surrounded Cross Bayou with the intent that someday, a dam could be built and re-create the "Great Raft" lake that existed before Captain Henry Miller Shreve drained it when he cleared the giant logjam in the 1830s. Cross Lake has been Shreveport's water source since 1927. He purchased more land west of the city and created the state fairgrounds as we know them today. He obtained funding and construction of the first non-railroad bridge across the Red River, from Shreveport to the new town of Bossier City.[130] John Henry Eastham died in Shreveport after a lengthy illness in November 1938. The *Shreveport Times* covered his death in a page-one headline story.[131]

CLARENCE AND CECILIA LEONARD ELLERBE

32°30″01.8347′N 93°43″54.2312′W
Block 12, Lot 1

Standing prominently in Block 12, Lot 1, near the southeastern corner of the intersection of Acacia Drive and Eastern Avenue in Greenwood, is the Ellerbe cenotaph. It guards the graves of Clarence Heber Ellerbe (1874–1937) and his wife, Cecilia Leonard Ellerbe (1880–1967). The monument is intricately carved from white marble and is designed in the Greco-Roman/ Egyptian Revival style.

The families of this couple defined the history of late nineteenth-century Caddo Parish and the progressive era of the early twentieth century in the region. Clarence Heber Ellerbe was born in Montgomery County, Alabama, in April 1874. He came to Shreveport in 1897 with the Louisiana Railway and Navigation Co., which later formed part of the Louisiana and Arkansas Railroad.[132] Clarence was the grandson of Nicholas Cobb, the first Episcopal bishop in Alabama.[133] He saw an opportunity in plantation agriculture and became a preeminent planter. Following a long decline in his health and a massive heart attack, his death was recorded as a page-one story by the *Monroe Morning World* on August 8, 1937.[134] Ellerbe Road and Leonard Road are named for the family. Although large holders diversified crops, Southeast Caddo Parish was and remained rich cotton land.

Clarence was married to Cecilia Leonard Ellerbe. She was born in December 1880. Cecilia was the daughter of Albert Harris Leonard

Clarence and Cecilia Ellerbe cenotaph.
Image by the author.

and Lucy Lee Howell Leonard of Greenwood in western Caddo Parish.[135] Albert Harris Leonard was the longtime owner and editor of the *Shreveport Times* and a planter in southeastern Caddo Parish. Lucy Howell Leonard was a descendant of the Howell/Atkins families who owned the extensive Forest Park Plantation west of the town of Greenwood.

Cecilia lived a life to be envied. She graduated from Sophie Newcomb College in New Orleans, was a widely published poet, served on the Caddo Parish School Board and was one of the founders of the Woman's Department Club in Shreveport. She served as a founding member of the Shreveport Little Theater. A champion of literacy, she served on the Shreveport Library Board. The *Shreveport Journal* noted on her passing, "As she recognized, the development of library facilities for public use is one of the most effective ways to raise the general educational level outside the classroom. She knew that both good schools and good library service were essential for the economic advancement of Caddo Parish."[136]

Clarence and Cecilia Ellerbe were stewards of the lands they controlled. They possessed deep connections with the economic health of Caddo Parish and the welfare of its people. They sought to make significant changes in the lives of others and had the drive and will to make them happen.

LAURA MAY FERGUSON

32°30"07.7964'N 93°43"52.8046'W
Unplatted Pay Row lot between Masons' Rest Lot 75 and Acacia Loop

LAURA MAY
Feb. 25. 1907
Mar. 28. 1909

———

BABY RUTH, infant
Daughter of
D.B. & DELLA
FERGUSON

———

Fold her, O Father, in Thy arms
And let her henceforth be
A Messenger of love between
Our human hearts and Thee.[137]

A popular motif in gravestones between 1890 and 1910 was the placement of the primary marble stone atop a sturdier stone of a different, darker and denser stone, usually granite. The typically incised base appeared hewn into a more complex shape. Laura May Ferguson's monument is an example. The stone is as poignant as her story. It lies on the west side of Acacia Loop adjacent to Lot 75 of Masons' Rest.

Laura May Ferguson's tombstone. *Image by the author.*

The *Shreveport Journal* reported Laura May Ferguson's story on the day following her death:

Little Girl Dies
Laura Ferguson, Aged 2 Years, Victim of Congestion
Laura Ferguson, two years old, daughter of Mr. and Mrs. Dave S. [sic] Ferguson, who reside on Laurel Street, died yesterday afternoon due to an attack of congestion and chicken pox. The parents did not realize the child was very sick until some hours after the first complaints. When Dr. A.S. Reisor, Sr., who was summoned, reached the house, the little girl was dying, expiring a little while later. The funeral was held this afternoon.[138]

Laura May's tombstone is made of white marble. Although beautiful, marble is susceptible to weathering, particularly from acid rain. As a result, the four-line epitaph is mainly illegible. Many iconographic symbols form the front and top of the stone. The lower portion of the marble displays ferns, which signify humility, frankness and sincerity.[139] Anchored from the top and opening to the ferns is a scroll that portrays the book of life. Appropriately, all text is located there. Most visitors who see this gravestone do not take time to examine it closely. Two baby shoes atop the stone hold down the scroll metaphorically. The left shoe's sole rests on the top of the monument. The right shoe is upside down, with the sole facing the visitor. This is a rare symbol of a life cut short. A companion horse at a military funeral may have boots facing backward in the stirrups. A cemetery column with an unfinished top conveys the same message.

Some researchers believed that the gravestone reflects burials of sisters. This is incorrect, as the *Shreveport Journal* story reflects. The problem is that Laura May was affectionately called Baby Ruth by her parents.

JEROME BONAPARTE GILMORE

32°30"04.9868'N 93°43"56.3471'W
Re-subdivision of Greenwood Cemetery Lot 22, between Block 33 and
Central Avenue

JEROME B. GILMORE
1827–1900

Jerome Gilmore is buried in Lot 22 in Planters' Rest near the intersection of Central Avenue and Garnet Street. He is buried near, but not in, the Confederate Veterans' Bivouac. Gilmore was born in Louisville, Kentucky, in 1827 and moved to Shreveport before the Civil War. The National Archives and the National Park Service list him as both J.P. Gilmore and Jerome B. Gilmore; the latter is correct.[140] His Civil War records are more complete than the great majority of entries. When he enlisted, Gilmore was elected captain, field and staff of Company F, the Shreveport Rangers of the Third Louisiana Infantry Regiment, on May 17, 1861, in New Orleans. He was with his unit until early 1862, when he was detailed to Fayetteville, Arkansas, under General Ben McCullough. Gilmore returned to the Third Louisiana in May 1862 and was elected lieutenant colonel that month. The Third Louisiana saw action during the Shiloh Campaign in Tennessee and Mississippi that spring, and Gilmore was wounded at the Battle of Iuka on September 19, 1862. He was then absent on furlough for recuperation. He returned to service for the Vicksburg Campaign in 1863 and led the Third

Jerome Bonaparte Gilmore.
Northwest Louisiana Archives, LSU-Shreveport.

Louisiana as its colonel. He surrendered on July 4, 1863, during the surrender of Vicksburg and was paroled two days later.[141] His formal record ends there.

He resigned his commission on July 7, 1863, and returned to Shreveport. Like many other Confederates, he immersed himself in politics.[142] He was a member of the General Leroy Stafford Camp No. 3 in Shreveport. His former rank in the Confederate officer corps certainly helped him. Gilmore ran for and was twice elected mayor of Shreveport from 1869 to 1871. This was during a transitional period in Reconstruction, but things spiraled downward quickly. The Radical Republican Henry Clay Warmoth became governor of Louisiana and immediately used federal troops to enforce his will.[143] Warmoth pronounced the duly elected mayor and councilmen to be illegally serving and appointed his own officials.[144] Soon after, he closed the *Shreveport South-Western* and set it up as a freedmen's newspaper. It lost all of its advertising, and the *Shreveport Times* began operations almost immediately. Gilmore was a local gunsmith before the war but did not return to that profession. He remained active as a cotton buyer for Herman Loeb in Shreveport until his health declined. He died on May 7, 1900.[145]

The family cenotaph is modern granite, and each person has a rectangular block with the names inscribed.

BURCH GRABILL

32°30"07.1246'N 93°43"52.0295'W
Spanish-American War Section, Row 1

Burch E
Grabill

-

Indiana

-

Corp.
45 U.S. Vol. Inf.
June 30, 1936
Camp Commander
1935

On the westernmost row of Spanish-American War veterans lies Burch E. Grabill.[146] He was a native of Wilmington, Ohio, and attended Quaker College in that city. There, he explored photography and thought it might be a profession.[147] He volunteered to fight in the Spanish-American War in 1898 and served in the Philippines as a military photographer. After his military service, Grabill moved to Fayetteville, Arkansas, and worked as the principal photographer for the University of Arkansas for fifteen years.[148] During World War I, he was posted to Camp Beauregard, near Alexandria, as a photographer. He came to Shreveport in 1919 and remained there for the rest of his life. He was a member of the W.H. Mabry Camp No. 14 of the Spanish-American War veterans, serving as the camp commander in 1935. His son William "Bill" Grabill worked with his father and succeeded him in the photography business in Shreveport. The signature on all of his photos (and those of his son) read, "Photo by Grabill." Burch Grabill died in 1936 and was buried with full military honors. His passing was covered in the *Shreveport Journal* with over three columns of space. The article best summed up his life: "He was unselfish and untiring in his service: in fact, he virtually gave himself to the community, often overtaxing his strength to serve others."[149]

Burch Grabill. *From McClure and Howe,* History of Shreveport and Shreveport Builders, *p. 315.*

Long after his death, Burch Grabill's work remains iconic. A book of the Grabills' work was published in 2003. *Photo by Grabill: A Legacy of Images: Burch and Bill Grabill's Northwest Louisiana* is a fitting tribute to the father and son who chronicled the region.[150]

VICTOR GROSJEAN

32°30"06.0144'N 93°43"54.6030'W
Confederate Veterans Bivouac, Lot 19

Victor Grosjean
Died in Shreveport
March 25, 1928
Man and Citizen
Loyal and Courageous
GROSJEAN

Lying on the east side of Confederate Veterans' Bivouac in Lot 19 is the grave of Victor Grosjean. He was a native of New Orleans, born there in 1844.[151] At age thirteen, Grosjean furthered his education in his spare time after his father died.[152] He was an avid reader and writer. As soon as Louisiana joined the Civil War, Grosjean enlisted and initially served as a private in Company A, First Louisiana Infantry Regiment, known as the Louisiana Guards.[153] The first units raised in Louisiana went east to guard recently occupied sea fortifications. Next, Grosjean and his unit went to Pensacola, Florida, and Virginia under General John Magruder.[154] After his short enlistment, he reenlisted and served under Colonel (later General) Henry Watkins Allen and the Feliciana Rifles. He rose through the ranks and was promoted to the rank of major. As the *Confederate Veteran* notes:

"From July 1862, young Grosjean was engaged in every battle of his regiment through the strenuous campaigns in Georgia, Tennessee, Louisiana, and Mississippi fighting gallantly to the end. His regiment surrendered to General [E.R.S.] Canby at Meridian, Miss., May 12, 1865."[155] He returned to New Orleans, but his health declined, and he moved to Shreveport. Grosjean was an honored member of the General Leroy Stafford Camp No. 3 of the United Confederate Veterans.

Victor Grosjean. *From McClure and Howe,* History of Shreveport and Shreveport Builders, *p. 261.*

Grosjean soon put his writing skills to work as a reporter, essayist and protagonist for the return of control in local affairs. He was very popular during the remainder of his life, and he wrote earnestly and honestly according to his principles for the next sixty years. History from the last years of the twentieth century forward has not been kind to him. *History of Shreveport and Shreveport Builders* correctly summed up Grosjean:

> *He was a moral crusader, and his honesty, integrity and sincerity was never questioned. He gave no thought to the accumulation of material things, but labored unceasingly and unselfishly to render service to his city, his parish, his state and to his country. And he did it effectively.*
>
> *He put principle above everything and he feared no man or set of men. When he entered into the conflict in which evil forces were arrayed against that which for the public good, he went into the battle with the full consciousness that truth would prevail, and he never looked back. He asked no quarter and he gave none.*[156]

Grosjean was a reporter for the *Shreveport Standard* and the *Shreveport Times* during Reconstruction. He dealt with the censorship of the federal forces in Shreveport until their withdrawal from northwest Louisiana in 1873 and 1874. Following the end of Reconstruction in 1877, he was a voice for what was known as the Redeemers or the Bourbons, the archconservatives who wanted to return to antebellum times. This effort was not to bring back slavery but rather to return the men who had held power to the *status quo ante*. He was the editor and co-owner of a new newspaper, *The Caucasian*, in 1890. He ran it for thirty-six years, and its intended purpose was to reverse "the evil effects of the reconstruction period following the Civil war period.... And the *Caucasian* was established especially to represent white supremacy in the South."[157]

Grosjean's stance on redemption has sadly been the only focus of his legacy. He was a moral crusader. He fought against the evil effects of the corrupt Louisiana Lottery. The leaders of the lottery tried to intimidate and then kill him in the first decade of the twentieth century.[158] He led the efforts during three prohibition campaigns to end the sale of hard liquor in Caddo Parish. He sold his newspaper interests in 1925 due to his declining health.[159] The *Shreveport Times* obituary ran as a news story. It began:

> *MAJOR VICTOR GROSJEAN*
> *Major Victor Grosjean is dead.*
>
> *This message which has caused a pall of sorrow to fall upon Shreveport, Caddo and all Louisiana. A great oak has fallen in the mighty forest and there will be none to take the place of that stalwart, fearless man who for many years made his influence felt by the power of his pen and alertness of his quickly discerning mind.*
>
> *Major Grosjean was a journalist of the old school. All his life he spoke freely his convictions, dealing fairly with friend and foe.*[160]

MILTON AND ETHEL HANCOCK

32°30″02.5843′N 93°43″56.5008′W
Block 29, Lot 2

A.D. 1893
Ethyl
1888–1892
Milton Taylor Hancock
1858–1905
Hancock

The first grand tomb built in Greenwood belongs to Milton Hancock and his young daughter, Ethel. The tomb's style was first seen in the mausoleum of Cyrus the Great, the king of Persia, at Pasargadae, Iran.[161] The Hancock tomb is an enigma, and many questions surround it. Milton Hancock was a self-made man. He made a large fortune by inventing and patenting the modern disc rotary plow that is still used today.[162] Hancock defended his patent against several individuals who attempted to usurp his legal ownership of the design. The tomb is located in Block 29, Lot 2, on the north side of Beryl Street.

Milton Hancock was something of a rogue. He claimed he was a southerner, but some accounts have indicated that he was born in Indiana and doing business there.[163]

Hancock's estate was thrown into turmoil following his death. The *Los Angeles Herald* reported:

BEGIN FIGHT OVER HANCOCK ESTATE: Claim manufacturer had two wives. Heirs appear in Superior Court.
Man Who Was Killed in Auto Accident Three Years Ago Owned Valuable Local Property
A contest over the estate of Milton Taylor Hancock, who was killed in an automobile accident on July 20, 1905, leaving an estate valued at $35,000, together with income from patents on his Benecla plow Invention amounting to $50,000 annually, was begun yesterday in the probate department of the superior court, when hearing was begun on the petition of Mollie Hancock McNatt and John P. Hancock to determine heirship.

They are opposed by Mrs. Nina Little-Hancock-Michelson, widow of the Inventor, and Milton Taylor Hancock, Jr., Eugenia Hancock and Newton Hancock, children of the couple.

The petitioners claim Hancock, when he married Mrs. Little, in 1886, already had a wife living in Georgia from whom he had not been divorced. Mrs. Michelson testified yesterday that she married Hancock in 1886, and the marriage license was placed in evidence. A large number of depositions from the alleged heirs in Georgia were also presented to the court.

Hancock was killed on North Main street when his automobile crashed into a milk wagon. Mrs. Hancock and the three children, who were in the machine at the time, were also badly injured.

Hancock was the Inventor of the disc plow, and was at the time of his death reputed to be immensely wealthy, receiving large royalties on his patents. He was an automobile enthusiast and was constantly endeavoring to reach the highest speed possible.

At one time he was a strong believer in spiritual manifestations, and as a result of what he claimed to be messages from the unseen world he erected one of the costliest monuments in the country at his beautiful home in Shreveport, La. Later he abandoned his faith in these teachings, paying $1000 to have the monument removed to a cemetery.[164]

The story is highly convoluted. After Hancock's business took off, he moved to Los Angeles with Nina Little, his second wife. The couple were socialites and spent extravagantly. After his high-speed collision with a milk wagon that killed him, the four children from his first marriage to Nancy Hiers Hancock, who died in 1902, sued the second wife and her surviving

Milton and Ethel
Hancock's mausoleum.
Image by the author.

children by Hancock. The first group contended that the Colorado divorce to Hiers was illegal and, therefore, the Arkansas marriage certificate was illicit.[165] The California Supreme Court sided with the second wife.

Milton Hancock had erected the mausoleum in the yard of his Shreveport home to serve as a memorial to his four-year-old daughter, Ethel. Both Milton and Nina Hancock believed that they could converse with and engage with their daughter. However, Nina had a stronger opinion on the matter than Milton. Nina sat in a chair inside the tomb and read to little Ethel every afternoon.[166] After Milton's death, she remained in Los Angeles; however, Milton's body was removed to Shreveport to be with Ethel. California records indicate that Nina remarried in Los Angeles and is buried there. Before his death, Milton moved the mausoleum from his yard to Greenwood Cemetery. Today, Ethel's cast-iron coffin with a clouded glass window remains in the tomb. There is another badly damaged iron coffin with wood lining in the tomb.[167]

A close reading of the inscription on the tomb shows that the Hancock tomb is older than the cemetery. The reason, of course, is that it served as a tomb, a memorial and a grand yard ornament.

JAMES FAIR HARDIN

32°30"04.9966'N 93°43"53.2290'W
Ascension Commandery Knights Templar Section, Lot 1

Col. James Fair Hardin
Oct 2, 1893–Oct 30, 1940

James Fair Hardin. *From Northwest Louisiana: A History of the Watershed of the Red River 1714–1937, Vol. 1, frontispiece.*

One of the finest historians ever produced in north Louisiana lies in Greenwood in an honored place in the Ascension Commandery Knights Templar section in Lot 1 at the southwest corner of the intersection of Turquoise Street and Western Avenue. Colonel James Fair Hardin (he preferred to be called J. Fair) lies in a family plot with his parents that features a relatively small columnar cenotaph resting on an octagonal base engraved with the family name. The individual tombstones give each person's information. Visitors are drawn to the unusual arrangement of stones.

He served as an assistant United States attorney for the Western District of Louisiana based in Shreveport. He earned a reputation for being scrupulously honest and ethical. When Governor Richard Leche and LSU president James Monroe Smith were indicted by the East Baton Rouge

Grand Jury in 1939, Hardin was selected as special assistant attorney general prosecuting the case.[168] The *Baton Rouge States-Item* described him perfectly:

> *J. Fair Hardin of Shreveport is a blunt, direct man, with an uncanny way of searching for the truth, and a disconcerting reputation for ferreting out crooks and bringing them to justice.*
>
> *Up in North Louisiana where they have known him since he first hung out a shingle, they say he's a whiz of a prosecutor and as "straight as a string." There are those who maintain that he'd "prosecute his own grandma if he caught her a-stealin" but Mr. Hardin himself, is apt to call this something of an exaggerated statement.*
>
> *His hair has a way of standing up straight from his head. His eyebrows sorta stand up in the same fashion. He stands the same way himself—straight. And there's something forceful and hard behind that straightness and that directness. It is reflected in his eyes. A crook—or even a good-sized grafter—wouldn't have much of a chance against a man like that.*[169]

The governor and the president were tried, convicted and sentenced to hard labor at Angola Prison.

Hardin simultaneously served as the colonel and organizer of the 204th Coast Artillery Regiment based at Fort Humbug in Shreveport. Following his death, the armory at Fort Humbug was named in his honor, and a copper box time capsule was cemented into a wall and a large bronze marker erected over the box. Among the items in the box are a copy of a special section of the *Shreveport Times* commemorating Hardin's life, orders of commendation for the regiment describing its lineage going back to the Civil War, resolutions of sorrow at Hardin's death passed by the First Presbyterian Church Bible Luncheon Club, the J. Fair Hardin Bible class at First Presbyterian, a general regimental order announcing Colonel Hardin's death and a roster of all members of the regiment who served under him.[170]

J. Fair Hardin's interests and knowledge seemed boundless. He served as the historian and cofounder of the Galvez Chapter of the Sons of the American Revolution in Shreveport in 1924.[171] He authored the historical plaques placed in the niches of the "new" courthouse in Shreveport in 1930.[172] He wrote a history of Louisiana courts of appeal in 1931,[173] and he delivered the first of ten lectures for the YMCA on the history of Louisiana in 1939, among many others.[174]

Hardin's magnum opus was the seminal *Northwestern Louisiana: A History of the Watershed of the Red River 1714–1937*, in three volumes.[175]

James Fair Hardin's ground tablet. *Image by the author.*

On October 29, 1940, J. Fair Hardin, driving himself, left Shreveport alone for a federal court trial in Monroe, Louisiana. Nine miles east of Minden on U.S. Highway 80, his car skidded off the road, overturned, rolled over several times and caused him to lose consciousness His skull was fractured, as well as four ribs.[176] An ambulance took him to the Minden hospital. He never regained consciousness and died at 3:35 a.m. the following day.[177] News of the wreck spread immediately across the state and beyond. Coverage of his death spanned many pages in the state's most influential newspapers.[178]

Hardin's stone contains his name and birth and death dates. Below this information are the seals of his most beloved organizations, the insignia of the Sons of the American Revolution and the 204th Coast Artillery Regiment.

REVEREND ROBERT JAMES HARP

32°30"04.9966'N 93°43"53.2290'W
Block 39, Lot 20

Robert James Harp
1829–1914

———

Methodist Circuit Rider for 68 Years
First Pastor of First Methodist Church 1846–1848
Pastor of Texas Avenue Methodist Church (Lakeview) 1901
First Pastor Noel Methodist Church 1906

———

"Well Done Good and Faithful Servant
Enter into the Joy of Your Master"

———

Agnes Pennington Harp
1843–1913

Reverend Robert James Harp lies in Block 39, Lot 20, just east of Western Avenue and south of Garnet Street. He was born in Lawrenceburg, Tennessee, in April 1829 and died in Shreveport in July 1914 at age eighty-five. At age seven, the young Robert Harp was orphaned and moved toward devotion early.[179] His eulogist, Reverend W.H. Wynn, president of Centenary College, stated, "We see the prophecy of his quenchless industry and independence of spirit in his early farm work and his ambition to 'plow like a man' when only eight years of age, his refusal to be dependent on others when eleven years and his studying even while he plowed during the day, his speller in the plow-handle."[180]

Reverend Robert James Harp. *From McClure and Howe,* History of Shreveport and Shreveport Builders, *p. 300.*

Reverend Harp played a significant role in Shreveport history, serving as the first pastor of Shreveport's First Methodist Church. At his death, Reverend Harp was the oldest member of the Louisiana Methodist Conference and perhaps the oldest Methodist minister in the southwest, having served as senior pastor and a circuit rider in Shreveport, Lake Charles, New Orleans, Lake Providence and Alexandria.[181] He received the call to the ministry early, at age fourteen, while still in his hometown of Lawrenceburg.

At age eighteen, Reverend Harp was in Louisiana by 1857, helping to organize the Louisiana Methodist Conference as a charter member.[182] He served briefly in service in the Confederate army in 1861, enlisting as a private in "New" Company G, Fourth Louisiana Infantry Regiment, on July 25, 1861, and discharged on December 28, 1861, probably as a six-month enlistment.[183] As he began his career in Louisiana in Shreveport, Reverend Harp helped build and minister in charges across Louisiana. He spent his final years at a mission church of First Methodist that became Noel Methodist Church in the Highland neighborhood.[184] Reverend Harp's last public appearance was a great one for himself, Louisiana Methodists and the city of Shreveport. He helped lay the cornerstone of the new First Methodist Church at the head of Texas Street, the location of the current complex.[185]

A few weeks before his death, Reverend Harp suffered a fall and rapidly declined when he contracted pneumonia.[186] The *Shreveport Journal* covered his death as a page-one news story the next day. The funeral service warranted a two-column-wide news story that referred to the minister as "this grand old man of God."[187] His total service to the Methodist Church spanned seventy-one years, sixty-seven of them in Louisiana.[188]

Reverend Harp lies with his wife, Agnes Pennington Harp, under a large etched granite monument.

WILLIAM KENNON HENDERSON JR.

32°30″03.3764′N 93°43″57.1951′W
Block 41, Lot 3

W.K. Henderson, Jr.
Aug. 6, 1880
May 28, 1945

Lying in Block 41, Lot 3, is the grave of William Kennon Henderson Jr. His monument is not glorious. This remarkable man was an industrialist, a maverick, a futurist, a progressive and a rogue. He captivated millions in the early twentieth century, all from the living room of his estate, Kennonwood, near Mooringsport in northern Caddo Parish or from his office. Henderson was a force to be reckoned with. At his death in 1945, the *New York Times* called him the "Stormy Petrel of Southern Broadcasting."[189]

W.K., as he preferred to be called, was born in Bastrop, Louisiana, in August 1880. He died in Shreveport in May 1945. During those sixty-four years, he changed life in America through broadcasting. He grew up in Jefferson, Texas, and attended Thatcher Institute in Shreveport before graduating from St. Edward's University in Austin, Texas. His family moved to Shreveport in 1896, and his father established the Henderson Iron Works and Supply Company in downtown Shreveport adjacent to Twelve Mile Bayou. The ironworks became the source of the family's great wealth. W.K. Jr. established the Henderson Garage and sold Ford automobiles. Henry Ford

William Kennon Henderson Jr. *Northwest Louisiana Archives, LSU-Shreveport.*

told Henderson he could use only Ford parts, and W.K. wired Ford to "go to hell."[190] Ford pulled the franchise, and Henderson bought a competitor, the Chandler franchise. Following his father's death in 1918, he took over the ironworks, and it became the largest ironworks south of St. Louis. [191]

Henderson was never happy doing one thing. However, he saw the power of a new public medium: the radio. He did not believe in rules and saw the individual's rights as predominant over government's. This made him the right man at the right time to change history. He bought a small local radio station, WGAQ, in 1922, with full ownership in 1925. He changed the call letters to KWKH (Kennonwood and his initials). He fought WWL in New Orleans and the Federal Communications Commission to request his broadcast from 1,000 to 50,000 watts, the origins of the term "clear-channel broadcasting."[192] Depending on weather conditions, KWKH could be heard all across the nation. Henderson kept no firm schedule, lectured, played music that his call-in listeners wanted to hear and railed against entrenched politicians, large government and chain stores.[193] Today, we would call him America's first "shock-jock." He was perhaps the first to play phonograph records on air and had a vast collection.[194]

Henderson signed off with variations of "Hello, World, Dog-gone Ya!"[195] or "HELLO, WORLD—This is KWKH at Shreveport, Lou-ees-i-ana. Shreve-port on the air, telling the world. Don't go 'way!"[196]

People would telephone in, send telegrams or send mail by the thousands each day. He reportedly received twenty to thirty thousand pieces of mail daily. As a result, the local telephone company was forced to add two dedicated long-distance operators to receive the five hundred to seven hundred long-distance calls each night. In addition, Western Union had to install a teleprinter to handle the 1,200 telegrams nightly.[197]

If comments were negative, Henderson loved it. A challenge from a man in Des Moines, Iowa, brought this:

> *What's the matter with you, you sawed-off, hammered-down, pusillanimous lollypop!*
>
> *Here you low down dirty pup, why didn't you sign your name? You're as yellow as this telegraph blank I have in my hand.*
>
> *Why in hell don't you turn the little knobs of your radio set? Every radio set has little knobs on it. You made an ass out of yourself by sending me this telegram.*[198]

Sometimes fate would add new adventures to the ever-aware entrepreneur. Henderson loved to drink coffee while on the air, and he remarked how good it was. Thousands of people called, wrote or telegraphed him asking what brand it was. Henderson seized on this and told everyone that it was his special blend, and they could buy it from him. He had a local coffee supplier sell him coffee in one-pound cans with the label "Hello World Coffee" with his photo on it. Henderson sold the cans for one dollar at a time when anyone could buy loose grounds for eight cents. He reportedly sold one million pounds.[199]

Ordinary people and government agencies tuned in to hear his views, and they were many. He did not mince words. He attacked the FCC, which he referred to as "crooks, skunks, and grafters."[200] The progressive politician Huey P. Long was an ally until they fell out in 1930. Henderson backed Al Smith against Franklin D. Roosevelt in the 1932 presidential election, and when FDR won, the new president went after Henderson. The FCC investigated Henderson and forced him to sell the station. He sold KWKH for $50,000.[201]

Henderson led an active lifestyle. The *Shreveport Times* reported at the time of his death that he was stung by a wasp several years before he died and never fully recovered. He was "almost completely inactive physically in his final years."[202]

DR. RANDELL HUNT FAMILY

32°30″01.0861′N 93°43″55.5513′W
Block 17, Lot 4

Randell Hunt	*Emily Halsey*
M.D.	*Wife Of*
	Randell Hunt
1865–1920	*1868–1946*

Located in Block 17, Lot 4, and in Lot 4 of a re-subdivision of Greenwood, due east and across Central Avenue from Dr. T.E. Schumpert's tomb, lies the Hunt family: Dr. Randell Hunt, his wife, children and a son-in-law. A contemporary of Dr. Schumpert's, Dr. Hunt played a vital role in Shreveport's medical history.[203] Dr. Hunt is buried along with his wife, Emily Halsey Hunt. Their double monument is art deco style. Unfortunately, all of the Hunt stones face west, causing problems for visitors searching for them on sunny days.

The Hunts had four daughters: Theodora Gaillard Hunt (1892–1904), Virginia Peyre Hunt Prothro (1894–1964), Emily Halsey Hunt Dickson (1896–1927) and Rhoda Tryon Hunt Keith (1899–1962). All are buried in Greenwood Cemetery.[204]

Emily Halsey Hunt married Samuel Allen Dickson. They are buried due east from her parents. The couple has tall monuments that are only fully appreciated from the east faces. The monuments are white marble and

Left: Randell and Emily Hunt's monument. *Photo by the author.*

Below: The Hunt daughters. *From left*: Theodora Gaillard Hunt, Rhoda Tryon Hunt, Emily Halsey Hunt and Virginia Peyre Hunt. *Courtesy of Susan Keith.*

exquisitely carved, resembling church tracery windows. While they may appear identical from a distance, they are not. Emily's monument is slightly taller and broader. Carved from a single piece of marble, the memorial displays the ornate ecumenical window with a bouquet of Madonna (Easter) lilies resting at the bottom of the window. One stem has partially fallen, and the elaborate inscription is carved beautifully behind it. Another stem has broken and rests at the base below. All of the flowers are in full bloom. Her inscription reads:

> *Emily Halsey Hunt*
> *Wife of*
> *Samuel Allen Dickson*
> *1895   1927*
> *"A ministering Angel, thou."*

Samuel Allen Dickson's monument is also carved into a church tracery window, but his is slightly smaller and much narrower. Ivy is carved at the base of the window. His inscription is not obscured and reads:

> *Samuel Allen Dickson*
> *April 6, 1890*
> *December 20, 1936*
> *He was a record of charity,*
> *courage, honor and integrity.*

Among the four daughters, Theodora has received the most attention in recent decades. She was eleven years old when she died of rheumatic fever. A false legend has been told over the years that she died when she fell from an upper window in the Logan mansion located on Austin Place, south of Oakland Cemetery. Perhaps a little girl died there, but it was not Theodora. She suffered from the effects of rheumatic fever for two and a half years prior to her death. Dr. Hunt, her father, tried everything he could think of to help his eldest daughter.[205] Her pain caused her great agony, and although it must have been devastating to them, her parents sent her to Hot Springs, Arkansas, to "take the cure." The trip to Hot Springs and treatments with warm mineral baths helped Theodora, but they could not save her. She died in Hot Springs on June 20, 1904. Her death certificate stated the cause of her death: "her heart stopped beating."[206]

Opposite, top: The Emily Hunt Dickson and Samuel Dickson monuments. *Image by the author.*

Opposite, bottom: Theodora Hunt's ground tablet. *Image by the author.*

Right: Emily Halsey Hunt and her daughter Theodora. *Courtesy of Susan Keith.*

Theodora's grave is located to the south of and in line with her sister Emily's. Only a flat ground tablet remains. A small angel statue stood in line with Emily's grand monument at one time.[207] The ground tablet reads:

> *THEODORA GAILLARD HUNT*
> *September 26, 1892–June 20,1904*
>
> *She lives _ our "Gift of God"*

During her time in Hot Springs, she was visited by her sisters and grandmother at least once. Theodora came home by train at least once. A touching photograph in the family collection shows Theodora with her mother. We know that Theodora was in Hot Springs for most of her last year on earth. The last known letter to her father from Arkansas was in August 1903.

Wytheville[208]
August 14 1903

My Dear Father—
I am well from tonsilitis but I am suffering with rheumatism so baddly that I hardly walk. And I hardly can hold the pen to write to you. I feel like an old woman. They tell me here to sleep with a pug dog And he will take the rheumatism instead of me but they have to kill the dog so I would not do such a cruel thing. Virginia Emily and I went with a party fishing and we went in wading and we went with a lieutenant and his brother and a few other children and we had such a good time.

Lieutenant Crocket got a pound of candy. We caught nine fish and lost fifteen and we did have such a good time. Father you are not afraid When we go fishing with a soldier? Do you father. And we crossed a swinging bridge. I do not like them one bit. The water was not deep and the fish were four inches long. Grand-Mother's birthday was August 9. She spent her birthday on the cool breezy gallery. I sleep sometimes three and four hours in the day. I got your letter and was so pleased. Father please send me the August St. Nicholas and my physiology. How are your eyes? I hope they are better. I think I have written you a long letter.

Your Dear Child
Theodora Hunt [209]

BUSH KILE JARRATT

32°30"05.7882'N 93°43"46.6907'W
Re-subdivision of Greenwood Cemetery, Lot 418

Jarratt
Elizabeth   *Bush K.*
1887   1981   *1880   1944*

Greenwood contains hundreds of monuments that take extra time to locate, but they are worth the effort. These are ground tablets built low to the ground and can be mowed over without damaging them. Some of the more famous people in Greenwood are buried under this type of monument, but they usually are grouped near a large family monument called a cenotaph. Jarratt and his wife, Elizabeth, lie adjacent to Acacia Drive just south of the Orthodox Greek section in Lot 418 in the re-subdivision called Greenwood No. 2.

Bush Kile Jarratt was born in Buena Vista, Texas, but he was reared in Shreveport. The *Shreveport Times* reported his death in a news article.[210] According to the article, Jarratt had worked for both the Shreveport Police Department and the Shreveport Fire Department "but recently has been chief machinist at Angola [Louisiana State Penitentiary]." Among the honorary pallbearers were noted attorney J. Bennett Johnson (father of the future senator), Shreveport fire chief S.J. Flores, Sheriff Tom Hughes and members of the Shreveport Fire Department.[211] Jarratt was an honorable man who died after a lengthy illness.

Bush Kile Jarratt's ground tablet. *Image by the author.*

The traveling electric chair. *Angola Museum.*

Another part of Jarratt's life that is interesting: Bush Kile Jarratt's father was James A. Jarratt, a Confederate sergeant in Company B of the Consolidated Crescent Regiment.[212] He fought at the Battle of Mansfield and left a personal account. James Jarratt moved to Texas after the war and worked in a sawmill. He lost his leg in an accident and became a preacher, moving to Shreveport about 1900. He married twice and had ten children, five by each wife.[213] Bush Kile Jarratt was a son of the second marriage. He grew up in a religious family and took devotion to heart.

Official hangman was one of Bush Jarratt's jobs for Shreveport and Caddo Parish.[214] Among his claims to fame was the execution of D.P. Napier, the "Butterfly Man," in 1934. After working for the City of Shreveport in public safety, he was offered a job at Angola State Penitentiary as the chief mechanic in 1940. One might think this was in the motor pool, but Jarratt was in charge of the electric chair for electrocutions. In that year, the State of Louisiana changed its method of executions from hanging to electrocutions. State law in Louisiana required that the death sentence be carried out where the crime was committed. The answer was a traveling electric chair, nicknamed "Gruesome Gertie," assigned to the chief electrician's executioner.[215] The Caddo Parish Courthouse was built to allow a 220-volt line to run separately to the seventh floor. Hangings were conducted there, and the traveling electric chair was brought up in the elevator and placed in the narrow hall beside the pipe run. The mobile execution van and the generator to run the electric chair were parked on the courthouse's west side.[216] Bush Kile Jarratt was a kind man who prayed with each prisoner before carrying out the sentence.[217]

JIMMY JOE

32°30"03.9859'N 93°43"44.5117'W
Chinese Section east of re-subdivision of Greenwood Cemetery, Lot 389

The Joe family cenotaph is an impressive granite structure located adjacent to the eastern fence of Greenwood, due east of Lot 389 and east of the junction of the Plasterers' and Cement Finishers' Rest and the Painters' Rest. It is not located in the commonly used paths, and therefore, it is less visited other than by family members. The location has nothing to do with the importance of the Joe family and Jimmy Joe in particular. The Joe family was synonymous with Chinese food in Shreveport. In 1948, Jimmy immigrated to Shreveport from Canton, China, at age thirteen.[218] His father, Kong, had entered earlier and established the Bamboo Restaurant at the intersection of Centenary Boulevard and Olive Street. People in the Highland neighborhood and across Shreveport welcomed the Bamboo, and it became a cultural institution. First, the Joes introduced egg rolls and won ton soup to Shreveport. Next, they introduced spicy beef, pork, chicken and duck dishes. Louisianans love spicy food, so the Bamboo was a hit. As time went on, new dishes were added, such as blackened chicken and the "tidbit platter" as an appetizer.[219] Jimmy Joe told the *Shreveport Times* in 1991, "As long as you're dedicated to the business and work hard at it and give people what they want and have a clean balance sheet, sooner or later customers are going [to come] back."[220]

Jimmy Joe and his daughter Amy, photographed at the Bamboo Restaurant in 1991. *Northwest Louisiana Archives, LSU-Shreveport.*

The Joe family cenotaph. *Image by the author.*

The Joe family worked closely together in the restaurant business. Jimmy went to Cornell University and received a BA in hotel and restaurant management. He served in the army for three years and then returned to Shreveport. He talked to the *Shreveport Times* in 1991 about working and his adult children coming back during the holidays:

> *The kids have all grown up in the place. Mary* [Jimmy's wife] *Joe says, "People used to kid us about having such big family, and we'd say, 'Oh yes, we're raising our own labor crew.'" Just like the customers, the kids come back to the Bamboo. "Last Christmas, they* [were] *all home, and I got the MBA waiting on tables," Joe boasts. "The lawyer was here as hostess, and the doctor* [a son-in-law] *was the busboy. He was cleaning tables!"*[221]

Jimmy died in 1997 at age sixty-three.[222] The Bamboo is now closed, but Highland remembers its good times.

The Joe family cenotaph is composed of highly polished brown granite. It is imposing without being overly ornate. It faces due west, which creates an optical illusion for the lucky visitor. If the sun is relatively low in the western sky and aligned to the west, the monument turns into a reflective mirror. The upper portion disappears, and the sky and clouds are perfectly reflected. The lower part catches the sun's rays, and the visitor or the landscape behind them appears. The cross and the name "Joe" seem to float.

RABBI DAVID LEFKOWITZ JR.

32°30"00.6410'N 93°43"46.7636'W
B'nai Zion Section, Lot 15D

RABBI DAVID LEFKOWITZ, JR.
AUG 8, 1911–FEB 6, 1999

יריקי החונמ ליל

The Hebrew inscription translates as
"Nights rest my darling/beloved/treasure"[223]

The grave of Rabbi David Lefkowitz Jr. is in the B'nai Zion section, Lot 15D. The handsome gray granite monument is simple in contrast to the greatness of the man who rests there. Rabbi Lefkowitz served the B'nai Zion congregation for almost fifty years and his city and his country as well. He had a keen mind, pleasant wit and clear vision of right and wrong. He fought antisemitism during World War II in Europe and at home. By the definition of nineteenth-century historian Thomas Carlyle, Rabbi Lefkowitz was a Great Man.

Rabbi Lefkowitz was born in Dayton, Ohio, in 1911, the son of Rabbi David Lefkowitz Sr. and Sadie Braham Lefkowitz. The family moved to Dallas, Texas, in 1920, when Rabbi Lefkowitz Sr. became the senior rabbi at the large Temple Emanuel.[224] Rabbi Lefkowitz Sr. served at Temple Emanuel until his retirement in 1948.[225] The young David Jr. attended university at the University of Texas before returning to his native Ohio. There, he earned a bachelor of arts degree at the University of Cincinnati and then his rabbinical orientation at Hebrew Union College, also in Cincinnati.[226] In 1937, he moved back to Dallas, where he served as the assistant rabbi at Temple Emanuel under his father.[227] He married Leona Atlas in 1938. Two years later, Rabbi Abram Brill, the rabbi at B'nai Zion in Shreveport, was in declining health, and that congregation asked Rabbi Lefkowitz Jr. to assist him. He moved to Shreveport in 1940, and Rabbi Brill almost immediately retired. Rabbi Lefkowitz became the eleventh rabbi to serve B'nai Zion since its founding in 1859.

Soon after Pearl Harbor was attacked in December 1941, Rabbi Lefkowitz volunteered for service in the U.S. Army Air Corps (soon to be the U.S. Army Air Force) and became a chaplain. However, he remained senior rabbi at B'nai Zion, with three rabbis filling in as assistants during his absence.

He first served in California, then in England and, later, in Germany. While in Germany, Rabbi Lefkowitz saw the ravages of the Allied bombing campaign and the horrific scenes of the Holocaust. His work with the air force in Germany widened substantially, taking him across western occupation zones. Rabbi Lefkowitz's ministry was of healing and remembrance of the six million Jews who died at the hands of the Nazis. At that time, no one knew how many people had perished, and the West was only then learning of the horrors of the extermination camps in the east.

Rabbi Lefkowitz blessed the remains and ashes of the forty thousand dead at Dachau Concentration Camp outside Munich. He also went to towns that had thriving Jewish communities until the Nazis destroyed the neighborhoods, corralled the residents into ghettos and then deported them to work or death camps. Most of Rabbi Lefkowitz's work was performed in the states of Franken and Bavaria. He led teams of Jewish chaplains, assisted by Christian chaplains, and reconsecrated synagogues that remained standing despite horrendous desecrations. Some towns saw their Jewish populations, although tiny, return. Rabbi Lefkowitz assisted these communities. Two of these municipalities stood out: Bad Kissingen and Bad Neustadt. Bad Neustadt's Jews were obliterated, and the synagogue was razed, but it held a treasure. A Christian farmer recognized the importance of the synagogue's Torah scroll (the five books of Moses) and hid the scroll in his barn beneath wooden floorboards all during the war. Since no worshippers were left, the farmer asked the rabbi to take the Torah back to Shreveport so that it could continue to be used in religious services. Rabbi Lefkowitz honored the request and returned

RABBI DAVID LEFKOWITZ, JR.
AUG. 8, 1911 - FEB. 6, 1999

ליל מנוחה יקירי

Above: Rabbi David Lefkowitz's monument. *Image by the author.*

Right: Rabbi David Lefkowitz. *Northwest Louisiana Archives, LSU-Shreveport.*

to Shreveport, where the "German Torah" was used at B'nai Zion until 1982, when it became too fragile for weekly use on the Sabbath. It remains on display in the chapel.

In 1946, Rabbi Lefkowitz returned to his duties at B'nai Zion and continued his education, earning a doctorate in theological studies from Pike's Peak Seminary. Rabbi Lefkowitz received an honorary doctorate from Hebrew Union College in 1952 and another from Centenary College in 1956. In recognition of his work outside his faith, Rabbi Lefkowitz and his wife received a brotherhood citation from the National Conference of Christians and Jews in 1971. In addition, an extremely rare award was given to Rabbi Lefkowitz by Pope John Paul II in 1989. The Order of Benemerenti medal is granted to clergy and laity members for service to the Roman Catholic Church. Rabbi Lefkowitz taught religion at Centenary College from 1978 to 1988. He was also director of volunteer services at Confederate Hospital in Shreveport (now the Louisiana State University Health Sciences Center).

Rabbi Lefkowitz retired from duties as the senior rabbi of B'nai Zion in 1972 but kept a busy schedule. He taught, lectured, helped in the community and was a much sought-after speaker. He authored an editorial in the *Shreveport Times* in September 1987 that summed up his beliefs in democracy, religious freedom and civic duty:

> *The road of faith in modern religion runs along and merges with the paths of reason and human need. Thus, it is not possible for religion, under the changed spiritual and intellectual outlook of our day, to impose its authority by threats of punishment in the hereafter or to resort to the arms of the state or states....The drive for freedom of religion has deeply impressed the conviction upon the conscience of men that no religion is true to itself unless it comes as the expression of the free personality.... For by freely assuming a genuine commitment to the divine law, which reveals itself within our spirits and within the spirit of humanity, we gain real inward freedom and secure the well-being of the peace which we and all mankind so deeply crave.*[228]

Rabbi Lefkowitz's health declined during the 1990s, and he died on February 6, 1999, a day after his sixty-first wedding anniversary. Many of his sermons and personal papers are located in the David Lefkowitz Jr. Papers, American Jewish Archives at Hebrew Union College in Cincinnati, Ohio.[229]

FRANK "LEFTY" LEONARDOS

32°30″06.6812′N 93°43″46.3757′W
St. George Greek Cemetery, Lot 136

"Lefty"
Elefterios
Leionardos
Sept. 13, 1923
Mar. 30, 1943
"Killed in Service
Of His Country"

Lying adjacent to the central walkway in Lot 136 of the St. George Greek Orthodox section and facing west is the marker of Frank "Lefty" Leonardos. This unusual stark white marble tombstone is engraved with a football in bas relief above his name. The sculptor fashioned the marble in a rounded art deco style.

Nineteen-year-old Leonardos died in a dynamite explosion while training at Camp Swift, Texas, on March 30, 1943.[230] Camp Swift was a training base and German prisoner of war camp in Bastrop County, Texas.[231] Frank, known as "Lefty" locally, was an all-state football hero who played at Fair Park High School in Shreveport before leaving school in February and entering military service.[232]

Former Grid Star Killed In Explosion

FRANK LEONARDOS

Left: Frank Leonardos's tombstone. *Image by the author.*

Right: Frank Leonardos. *From the* Shreveport Times, *"Former Grid Star Killed in Explosion," April 1, 1943, 1.*

Oddly, the tombstone does not list his first name as Frank. Instead, "Lefty" is in quotes and below it "ELEFTERIOS" ("Lefty" in Greek). Below the birth and death dates, the inscription reads, "Killed in Service of His Country." Wartime necessities required a lack of information about the cause of death other than that listed. Lefty was a local celebrity. The *Shreveport Times* news story covering his death, featured on page 1, included a large photo of the young man in his football uniform, ready to throw the ball.

LSUMC

32°30"06.6812'N 93°43"46.3757'W
Northern extent of Oleander Avenue

L.S.U.M.C.
Donors
To Medical Science
Mortui Vivos Docenti
(The Dead Teach the Living)

The northernmost monument in Greenwood, at the northern end of Oleander Avenue, is also one of the most interesting. It marks the Willed Body Donor Program administered by the Department of Cellular Biology and Anatomy at the Louisiana State University Health–Shreveport, a teaching hospital.[233] Anyone living in northern Louisiana, eastern Texas or southern Arkansas can donate their body to science through this program. A core practice of medical education includes work on cadavers. Many medical fields use cadavers, including nursing, allied health and many disciplines of surgery. Bodies are used to perfect new surgical

LSUMC monument. *Photo by the author.*

techniques or examine new diagnostic methods.[234] Once the body has yielded all information gathered, it is cremated. If the family requests the ashes for later burial, that option is granted. If relatives do not make such a request, the ashes are gathered for burial in this plot. A dignified, appropriate ceremony occurs.[235]

DESSIE ALBERTA PHILEN MARTIN

32°30″03.1951′N 93°43″46.2296′W
Bricklayers' Union, Lot 226

The one who never lets us grow
Beyond the childhood stage,
Whom fond affection would bestow
Regardless of our age.
OUR   MOTHER

On the back:

> *DESSIE ALBERTA MARTIN*
> *APRIL 4, 1890*
> *JULY 11 1941*
> *"None knew thee but to love thee*
> *None named thee but to praise."*

Greenwood contains a wide variety of monuments, memorials and stones that reflect the personalities of the deceased. They often indicate the memories and perceptions of those left behind. One such remarkable marble memorial is located in Lot 226 of the Bricklayers' Union Rest. It is neither large nor imposing. The monument marks the grave of Dessie Alberta Philen Martin. She was born on April 4, 1890, and died on July 11,

Above: Dessie Alberta Philen Martin's monument. *Image by the author*.

Left: Detail of the Martin monument. *Image by the author*.

1941. Visitors are drawn to the information on the back of the stone. By its shape, it looks like a home with a hipped roof. At the center is a set of Dutch doors with the name "MARTIN" above them and a porcelain photo of Mrs. Martin. On either side are carved windows, and in the front of the doors is a welcome mat. On the roof is an epitaph that reads, "The one who never lets us grow/Beyond the childhood stage,/Whom fond affection would bestow/ Regardless of our age. OUR MOTHER."

The children wanted visitors to see what was most important about their mother. She was caring and welcoming, kind and gracious. After absorbing this and walking around the little house, visitors discover an inscription on the roof: "DESSIE ALBERTA MARTIN/APRIL 4, 1890/JULY 11 1941." The rear of the house includes another epitaph: "None knew thee but to love thee/ None named thee but to praise."

SAMFORD BROWN McCUTCHEN

32°30"04.2942'N 93°43"45.1469'W
Ascension Commandery Knights Templar Section, Lot 48

Samford Brown
McCutchen
July 9, 1834
July 18, 1913
I Have Fought the Good Fight
I Have Finished My Course
I Have Kept the Faith. II Timothy IV.7

Samford Brown McCutchen's grave lies in the Ascension Commandery Knights Templar section in Lot 48. The monument is finely etched in brilliant white marble. He served as a second lieutenant in Company I, Twenty-Seventh Louisiana Infantry Regiment, known as the Caddo Confederates. The unit saw service in the Vicksburg Campaign and was particularly effective in repulsing the Union attacks on May 19, 1863. This regiment was primarily composed of northwest and north-central Louisiana men. McCutchen made contacts in this regiment after the war as a member of the General Leroy Stafford Camp No. 3 of the United Confederate Veterans. He was born in Columbus, Georgia, in 1834 and moved to Shreveport before the Civil War. He remained in Shreveport for the remainder of his life, dying there in 1913 at age seventy-nine.[236] Soon after the Civil War, McCutchen decided on a course of action that would affect Shreveport for many decades. He could have become a planter and bought cheap rural land. Instead, he saw a niche in providing banking services. He was not the first to do this in Caddo Parish, but he was among the most successful.

McCutchen began as a bookkeeper and saved his money. In 1883, he bought into a small bank that became McWilliams, McCutchen and Deming.[237] He realized that a much larger institution would help large planters. In 1886, along with partners, he organized Commercial National Bank. He served as vice president until 1892, left Commercial and created Citizens National Bank. McCutchen retired from Citizens, and the bank changed its name to Louisiana Bank and Trust Company. He came

Samford Brown McCutchen. *From McClure and Howe,* History of Shreveport and Shreveport Builders, *p. 241.*

out of retirement and served as president of LB&T. He also helped organize the American National Bank. None of his banks failed. The citizens of Caddo Parish, not only large planters, benefited from his business acumen, and Shreveport benefited from his expertise. He helped organize and run Shreveport's street railway system.[238] Further, he was elected to the Caddo Parish School Board and was a member of First Methodist Church, serving as the chairman of the Board of Stewards.[239] He died in 1913, four years after the death of his wife, Amelia. Their joint succession totaled $326,704, a vast amount by today's standards.[240] McCutchen's tombstone sums up his philosophy and his life.

HAROLD AND CAROLYN MUROV

32°30"01.1800'N 93°43"45.4123'W
B'nai Zion Section, Lot 3F

Murov

Harold	*Carolyn*
Jan. 14, 1913	*Oct. 3, 1927*
Jan. 2, 2007	*July 26, 2020*

Located in the B'nai Zion section, Lot 3F, is the double brown granite tombstone of Harold and Carolyn Murov. The Murovs were well-known, respected members of the community. Harold was born in Brooklyn, New York, and grew up in Shreveport.[241] He graduated from C.E. Byrd High School in Shreveport and later served in World War II. He co-owned and managed Star Furniture on Texas Avenue in Shreveport with his father and brother. Harold was a Master Mason, holding membership in Lodges 115 and 432. Harold passed away in 2007 at age ninety-three. Carolyn Friedenthal Murov was born in Los Angeles, California, but lived in Shreveport almost all of her adult life. She was active in the life of B'nai Zion Temple, serving as president of the congregation and its temple sisterhood. In addition, Carolyn was active on the board of directors of the Shreveport Symphony and served as president of the Symphony Guild.[242]

The Murovs were a loving couple and were loved by family and friends. The author had a special relationship with Harold, who audited history

Harold and Carolyn Murov's double monument. Note the stones on the monument; visitors to Jewish graves leave stones instead of flowers. They show permanence and respect. *Image by the author.*

classes at LSU-Shreveport for the last decade of his life. Harold enrolled in almost every advanced history course that the author taught. He had a wry wit, and the students adored him. Once, in a course on the American Civil War, Harold proclaimed proudly that when he was in service in World War I, his artillery and cavalry units used the same tactics. The students were amazed. Finally, the question was asked how old he was during the Great War. He responded with a mischievous smile that he was very young and finally said he joined at age four. He knew enough about the subject to teach the class. The author had the pleasure of lecturing at the Oaks of Louisiana in Shreveport several times as part of its series "The University at the Oaks." Carolyn was a resident there in her later years and always attended, asked questions and offered keen insight into the topic each time.

MARTHA ELIZABETH
SEGURA NABORS

32°30"04.0230'N 93°43"41.2419'W
Masons' Rest, Lot 240

Martha Elizabeth
Segura Nabors
Oct. 23, 1954
Dec. 23, 2019
"Dance Then, Wherever
You May Be"

Martha Elizabeth Segura Nabors lies in the Masons' Rest section, Lot 240. She was born in Mansfield, Louisiana, on October 23, 1954, the fun-loving youngest of three, born to Mary (Murrell) and Jerry Taylor Segura. After graduation from Mansfield High School, she attended Northwestern State University, ultimately graduating with a degree in general studies. While there, she was a member of the Phi Mu fraternity. Martha moved to Shreveport early in her career, working as a petroleum landman. She originally lived in the Highland neighborhood and later

in Broadmoor. During a downturn in oil and gas, she began a career in sales, which led to a position with Planters Lifesavers. She left Shreveport when she accepted a district manager job in the Houston area for that company. While in Texas, she married and gave birth to two sons. Wanting to be closer to family, she returned with her husband and sons to Shreveport, where she owned and operated Nabors Insurance.

Her obituary summed up her personality and interests:

> Martha never met a stranger and turned many of them into friends. Her joi de vivre was evident to all. The only thing she loved more than her family was a good party with plenty of food, beverage, music and laughter. She found all of those things and more with her Mardi Gras Krewe des Ambassadeurs, which widened her circle of friendship. Community involvement was an important part of Martha's life. She was a member of the Salvation Army Women's Auxiliary, BNI Elite, Northwest Louisiana Association of Realtors, Women's Council of Realtors, Friends of a Feather and Muses at Centenary college. She was a diplomat for the Greater Shreveport Chamber of Commerce and was a 2019 nominee for the Shreveport Chamber group's Athena Award. Martha also supported animal welfare organizations as she had two rescue fur babies, Jack and Holly.[243]

She died after a brief illness just two months after her sixty-fifth birthday. Martha's monument is etched granite. Sometimes friends and loved ones leave tributes at grave sites in Greenwood. The winged metal heart in an empty sparkling wine bottle was left for her on New Year's Day 2022 in celebration of her life.

Opposite: Martha Elizabeth Segura Nabors's tombstone. *Image by the author.*

DANIEL BRYAN "BUNCE" NAPIER

32°30″12′N 93°43″53′W (Approximately)
Paupers' or Potters' Field

Like most large municipal cemeteries, Greenwood contains an area known as the Potters' Field or "Place of the Friendless." People indigent or unidentified find their final rest here, buried at public expense, most without fanfare. Others who commit foul crimes and become what was termed in the 1930s "public enemies" sometimes end up here too. Shreveport's first known serial murderer is buried in the Potters' Field. Located east of the northern extent of Oleander Avenue in the low area is a lawn with few tombstones. Somewhere under that lawn, with no memorial of any kind, lies Daniel Bryan Napier. He was also known locally as Fred Lockhart but most famously was called the "Butterfly Man." Napier's arrest and behavior were covered nationally in the spring of 1934 for an entire week before other tantalizing stories drove it from front-page headlines.[244]

The Great Depression gripped America and sent millions of people into poverty. Thousands of these folks found rapid transit by illegally catching rides on freight trains. Although most were honest, others were criminals and used the trains to escape the law. Daniel Napier was one of the latter. He grew up in Georgia. His sister was married to a former attorney general in Georgia, but no one knew that at the time. Napier, age thirty-eight, lived in a handmade shanty near Cross Lake in the woods off Dilg League Road with a common-law wife named Armor Anderson.[245] The couple had lived in

Left: Daniel Bryan Napier. *Northwest Louisiana Archives, LSU-Shreveport.*

Right: A butterfly ornament. *Northwest Louisiana Archives, LSU-Shreveport.*

Shreveport since mid-1933. "Lockhart" was well known locally because he frequented downtown and the riverfront, where he sold handmade papier-mâché or cloth butterflies secured with a hairpin. Women who worked downtown thought they were pretty ornaments and bought them.

What no one in Shreveport knew about Napier, perhaps not even his common-law wife, was that he had a mean, sadistic streak. Napier was convicted of being the driver for a lynch mob that killed Leo Frank, who was convicted of murdering a girl in 1914.[246] However, his brother-in-law pulled strings, and the sentence was changed from death to life in prison. The girl's murder was almost identical to a second one in Shreveport. Leo Frank was Napier's second murder. His third murder, in the same manner as his first, was Armor Anderson's son, Ligon Jackson, in Ferriday, Louisiana.

Napier used a knife as his primary weapon. In April 1934, Napier lured a fifteen-year-old bride-to-be named Mae Giffin into the woods near the "Hobo Jungle" where he lived. He raped her, slashed her throat and butchered her like a hog. He tried to burn the body but was not successful. The body was found, and evidence quickly pointed to Napier. The local newspapers thoroughly covered the murder and arrest. The wire services picked up the lurid story. It was carried by newspapers and radio from coast to coast. The public was enraged, but according to the *Shreveport Journal*, "the crowd was variously estimated at between 4,000 and 5,000, but only about two hundred…formed the actual mob…gathering about the courthouse square shortly after the *Shreveport Journal* with an extra edition, early Tuesday night [April 17] spread the news of the murderer's confession."[247] The mob broke through the police cordon and stormed the courthouse, only to be driven back by tear gas, sparklers and fire hoses.[248] The National Guard was brought in from Fort Humbug, the local armory, and restored peace.[249]

Napier's trial began at 9:00 a.m. on Monday, April 23. Spectators were allowed on a first-come, first-served basis. Members of the National Guard marched through the aisles and blocked all entrances as a preventive measure against any possible uprising. Machine guns were mounted in the lobby, while special "gas squads" stood nearby for use in the first line of defense.[250] The jury was empaneled by 11:00 a.m. The case was closed and sent to the jury by 1:13 p.m. The verdict was rendered five minutes later.[251] Napier was hanged on the seventh floor of the Caddo Parish Courthouse at 12:09 p.m. on May 18.[252] The story was at the top of national headlines for a week until the outlaws Bonnie Parker and Clyde Barrow were killed in Bienville Parish, about sixty miles to the east. Shreveport owed Napier a burial, but there would be no tombstone or flowers to mark his grave. Citizens wanted to forget that he ever existed.

Napier was the last person legally hanged in Caddo Parish.[253] Other people were later executed on the seventh floor of the Caddo Parish Courthouse, but they died by electrocution in the state's traveling electric chair.

RICHARD WILLIAM NORTON FAMILY

32°30″08.7501′N 93°43″52.9710′W
Masons' Rest, Lot 80

The Norton family plot, located in Masons' Rest, Lot 80, occupies part of the high plateau west of the veterans' lots section. The plot contains three graves: Richard William Norton (1886–1940); his wife, Annie Miles Norton (1886–1975); and an infant daughter born in 1917. The graves are marked with flat ground tablets, but the tremendous curved black granite bench cenotaph is striking in its elegance.

The Norton family was listed in the 1920 census as living at 2525 Fairfield Avenue at the corner of Robinson Place.[254] Richard's occupation was listed as an attorney. The 1930 census records them at the same address, but his occupation was "oil driller."[255]

This family has given much to the city and region that nurtured them. Richard William Norton, a native of Tennessee, was an attorney and oilman based in Shreveport and San Antonio. He was among a small group of oil pioneers who discovered and drilled the Rodessa Oil Field in the 1930s. Rodessa, near the town for which it is named, was one of the largest producing fields in the nation. When America was reeling from the Great Depression, workers found jobs in northwest Louisiana and northeastern Texas. Norton could have hoarded his money during those dark years, but instead, he became a philanthropist and investor. In 1940, R.W. Norton was in Texas to serve as a delegate in support of Franklin Delano Roosevelt's

The Norton family plot. *Image by the author.*

third term at the Democratic National Convention. He died there after suffering a heart attack.[256] Norton was a supporter and close friend of Vice President John Nance Garner, who sent flowers and condolences but could not attend the funeral.[257]

Annie Miles Norton and her son, Richard William Norton Jr., carried on R.W. Norton's philanthropic mission by creating the R.W. Norton Art Gallery and the Norton Art Foundation. The Norton, as many locals refer to it, is a world-class institution. Among its vast collections is the second-largest media collection created by Frederic Remington, including oil paintings, drawings and sculptures. It also holds the third most extensive art collection created by Charles M. Russell. Hudson River School works by Albert Bierstadt, Thomas Cole and Asher Durand grace exhibit halls, while Paul Revere's silver is also displayed. One room contains six huge sixteenth-century Flemish tapestries. Cases holding rare firearms contest with the museum's doll collections. The museum features a casting of Rodin's *The Thinker* and other sculptures inside and in the surrounding botanical gardens. The map library, closed to the public, houses extremely rare maps and folios.[258] The Nortons also conduct educational lectures, series for children and oral histories of veterans equal to even the Smithsonian Institution. Mrs. Norton, whose son, Richard William Norton Jr., preceded her in death, died in Colorado Springs, Colorado, following a lengthy illness.[259] Funeral services were held at the Norton home on Fairfield Avenue.[260] Dr. J. Frank Alexander, pastor of First Presbyterian Church of Shreveport, officiated.[261]

Richard William Norton's entrepreneurial prowess and his wife and son's dedication to him and his mission make the R.W. Norton Art Gallery the region's crown jewel of museums. The current family members honor this treasure and make it accessible to all, free of charge.

WILLA NORWOOD

32°30"08.9113'N 93°43"51.8745'W
Spanish American War Section, Row 2

Willa S. Norwood
Nurse
U.S. Army
Sp. Am. War

Willa Norwood. *From the* Shreveport Times, *February 6, 1938, 4.*

Amid the rows of Spanish-American War graves lies Lieutenant Willa Stevens Norwood. The young Stevens was one of only forty members of the U.S. Army Nursing Corps who served during that brief but intense war. Norwood graduated from nursing school at the Medical College of Ohio (now the University of Cincinnati College of Medicine) and immediately enlisted. She trained at Fort Thomas, Kentucky. Upon completing her military nurse training, she earned the rank of lieutenant. All forty nurses met in New York and traveled on a transport ship to San Juan, Puerto Rico. Typhoid fever raged across the island. The U.S. Army barracks held four hundred cases. Throughout the war, Lieutenant Norwood remained at this facility and returned on the last troopship in 1899. Upon her return to the United States, she was in charge of nurses at the McCoy Sanitarium in Jackson, Tennessee, where she met her husband, Arthur Guy Norwood. The couple moved to Shreveport in 1915. She played a central role in the Woman's Christian Temperance Union and the Women's Auxiliary in the local W.H. Mabry Camp, United Spanish-American War Veterans. Her health declined slowly during the 1930s. She spent the last months of her life at the Schumpert Sanitarium.[262] Her husband died in 1943, and his grave is next to hers. Her gravestone contains the incised shield of a veteran of the Spanish-American War. Mr. Norwood's stone has no embellishments, indicating that he is buried there through his wife's service.

NANCY AND LARRY PLANCHARD

32°30"00.8696'N 93°43"45.8535'W
B'nai Zion Section, Lot 265

Larry's Inscription (Facing East):

Lawrence Joseph
Planchard, M.D.
October 21, 1976–June 12, 2007
Loving Son, Brother and Friend
Compassionate Doctor, Skilled Surgeon
Brilliant Ophthalmologist
Inquiring Mind with a Passion for Learning
From Art and Music to Esoteric Scientific Topics
Expert on World War II History
Master Model Builder
Talented Artist
Private Pilot with Life-Long Interest in Aviation
Loving Spirit, Fiercely Loyal
Wry Wit and Sense of Humor

Your passing has left an unspeakable void in our world.
Your beautiful smiling face will NEVER be forgotten.

Loved and missed forever by
Dad, Mom, Brian, Jeffrey and Emily

Larry's Inscription (Facing West):
> *Planchard*
> *Louisiana School for Math, Science and the Arts May 1994*
> *Washington University in St. Louis May 1998*
> *Bachelor of Science in Chemical Engineering*
> *Tulane University School of Medicine May 2002*
> *Doctor of Medicine*
> *Tulane University School of Medicine July 2002–June 2003*
> *Surgical Internship*
> *Louisiana State University in New Orleans Health Science Center*
> *Department of Ophthalmology July 2004–June 2007*
> *Resident in Ophthalmology*

At the lower right of the panel is an image of Larry's beloved dog, Charlie. The inscription reads:
> *Charlie*
> *Feb. 19, 2004*
> *Sept. 10, 2008*

Nancy's Inscription (Facing East):
> *Nancy Michele Herman*
> *Planchard*
> *February 18, 1951–August 12, 2011*
> *Loving Wife of 37 years to Dr. Thomas Planchard*
> *Beloved mother to Larry, Brian, Jeffrey, & Emily*
> *Nancy was the best wife and mother ever.*
> *She was beautiful inside and out and had a brilliant mind.*

Nancy's Inscription (Facing West):
> *1969 Graduate Hunting High School Huntington, WV*
> *1973 Bachelor of Arts H. Sophie Newcomb College of Tulane University*
> *Practice Administrator Bossier Ophthalmology Clinic 1981–2011*

The B'nai Zion section of Greenwood contains many beautiful monuments. A double memorial near the top of the list can easily be seen from Stoner Avenue and the small eastern gate. It is located in Lot 265. These stones are carved in pure black Indian granite. Here lie Lawrence "Larry" Joseph Planchard, MD, and his mother, Nancy Michele Herman Planchard. Regardless of size and quality, few tombstones depict lives as fully as these

Larry and Nancy Planchard's monument facing east. *Image by the author.*

two. Images of the mother and son are etched into the granite, which features detailed information about these two whose lives were cut short.

Larry was born in New Orleans and raised in Shreveport, the eldest of four children. He was a brilliant scholar with many interests. Larry was a chemical engineer, a general surgeon and an ophthalmologist. In addition, he was a first-rate historian and a master scale modeler. His love for learning was punctuated by a terrific sense of humor. Larry was fiercely dedicated to his family. At age thirty, he died of a sudden illness just before joining his father's practice.[263]

Nancy was a native of Huntington, West Virginia, and graduated from H. Sophie Newcomb College of Tulane University with a double major

Larry and Nancy Planchard's monument facing west. *Image by the author.*

in mathematics and art. She met her future husband, Thomas Planchard, who became a United States Air Force officer, an engineer, a surgeon and an ophthalmologist. The couple came to the area when her husband was transferred to Barksdale Air Force Base. At the time of her death, they had been married for thirty-seven years.[264] Nancy was an enthusiastic Saints football fan and traveled with her family to see as many home games as possible. She was also the glue that kept the Planchard family members and her husband's ophthalmic practice in order. She was funny, articulate, loving and wise beyond her years.[265] In the last seven months of her life, Nancy battled a vicious brain tumor, which resulted in her death.[266]

MICHAEL ROACH

32°30″03.0783′N 93°43″52.9219′W
Block 5, Lot 3

Born In   *Died In*
Ireland   *The Dispensing*
            Of His Duty
1847   *1899*
        Michael
         Roach

Among the many ornate monuments in Greenwood is an outstanding example of a cruciform (in the shape of a cross) tree stone. The complex carving is the gravestone of Michael Roach, a native of Ireland and the first professional firefighter to die in the line of duty in Shreveport.[267] During the city's greatest crisis, Michael Roach came to Shreveport from Cincinnati, Ohio, and served as a nurse during the yellow fever epidemic of 1873. In November of that year, the epidemic ended, and Peter Youree hired him to manage his streetcar stable. The streetcar system consisted of horse- or mule-drawn trolleys before electrification. Upon Roach's death, Youree told the *Shreveport Times*, "If Mike left, the streetcars would have to stop running."[268] Roach worked for the streetcar line until 1885, at which time he joined the Shreveport Fire Department.

Michael Roach's tree stone. *Image by the author.*

The fire department answered a call on the night of February 4, 1899. Roach was riding in a horse-drawn "chemical engine" (what we would call a foam truck) when it passed over a "very rough place in the street."[269] Roach was thrown from the engine. He suffered from two broken ribs, and the physicians at Dr. T.E. Schumpert's sanitarium (hospital) believed he might have other internal injuries. He appeared to be healing rapidly, but Roach died in his sleep on the evening of February 15. The doctors told the *Shreveport Times* that the fireman had just recovered from a severe attack of grip (influenza), which may have weakened his heart.[270] His death led the city to create a section for firefighters who died in its service. Block 5 was divided into six lots. Roach's grave occupies Lot 3 in the section that was named Fireman's Rest. It is unclear whether the magnificent monument was donated in whole or in part by the City of Shreveport or from Roach's three bank accounts totaling $2,279. There was no will, and he had no known heirs. Every square inch of the monument is covered in iconography or messages. The upper base appears as two carved stones containing the text "Born in Ireland 1841" and "Died in the dispensing of his duty 1899." The middle stone gives his name, "Michael Roach." The lower left stone has an engraved fireman's crossed ladder, shovel and helmet. The lower right stone contains an engraved Masonic symbol with a square, a compass and a traditional "G" in the middle. Above the base is an ornately carved marble cross portrayed by logs entwined by ivy. The ivy denotes everlasting life, and the cross signifies Christianity.

DR. THOMAS EDGAR SCHUMPERT

32°30″01.7831′N 93°43″56.2155′W

T.E. SCHUMPERT

The mausoleum of Dr. Thomas Edgar Schumpert commands the visitor's attention when entering Greenwood's main gate. The plot covers Block 27, Lot 5, and Lots 6 and 7 of a later re-subdivision. Similar to the nearby tombs of Milton and Ethel Hancock and Lucy Elmore Atkins, the Schumpert tomb is reminiscent of the mausoleum of Cyrus the Great, king of Persia, at Pasargadae, Iran.[271] The crypt is found behind large metal doors behind iron-grilled gates.

Dr. Schumpert's career in Shreveport began as a physician and surgeon at Charity Hospital, located at Moss Side Park, at the intersection of Ford Street and Pierre Avenue.[272] It grew from a Reconstruction-era military hospital. Shreveport built a new hospital that opened in 1889 at the northwest corner of Texas Avenue and Murphy Street, the city hall site in the last half of the twentieth century.[273] Dr. T.E. Schumpert was the surgeon in charge beginning in 1894.[274] He founded the Shreveport Sanitarium in 1894 using a former girls' school and created a nursing school there in 1898.[275]

Upon Schumpert's death in 1908 at age forty-six, he left a large sum of money to operate the hospital. As a result, the Shreveport Sanitarium became the T.E. Schumpert Memorial Sanitarium, located on Margaret Place. It was administered by the Sisters of Charity of the Incarnate Word until 1999, when that organization joined with other orders to become Christus.[276]

Above: T.E. Schumpert's mausoleum. *Image by the author.*

Left: The Schumpert angel. *Image by the author.*

The Schumpert tomb features Dr. Schumpert's name above the doorway. He shares it with his father, John Ira Schumpert (1835–1912), and his mother, Mary Pauline Holt Schumpert (1840–1898).[277] The tomb is within sight of the two other large Cyrus-like structures. A large, majestic angel guards it from the roof, similar to the Atkins tomb. The Schumpert angel is seated, her wings behind her and not spread. Her eyes are closed as if in thought. Her left hand holds a laurel wreath, symbolizing victory, eternity and immortality.[278]

ALBERT COLWELL STEERE

32°30"07.1638'N 93°43"53.6728'W
Masons' Rest, Lot 27

The man who created much of the twentieth-century residential landscape in Shreveport is found in Masons' Rest, Lot 27. Albert Colwell Steere was born in Shreveport in 1879. A.C. Steere was a visionary developer, entrepreneur and firm supporter of this region who served as a director of the Shreveport Chamber of Commerce.[279]

Albert Colwell Steere. *Northwest Louisiana Archives, LSU-Shreveport.*

Steere partnered with his father to buy and develop land and build streets, homes and sometimes businesses, expanding Shreveport to the south and east. The Steere Land Company was the core of the ventures, but they created other companies to handle financing and management of new neighborhoods. Among the firms were the South Highlands Company, the Caddo-Bossier Land Company, Steere Mortgage and Investment Company and the Broadmoor Golf Club.[280]

South Highlands was a town before being annexed into Shreveport in 1927. Steere and his friend Elias Goldstein built a large park and donated it to the Town of South Highlands. They named the park after their daughters, Betty Goldstein (Franklin) and Virginia Steere (Marston), and it is still known as Betty Virginia Park.[281] Another visionary project became the Tri-State Broadcasting System, which became KTBS Radio and, later, KTBS Channel 3 television. KTBS stands for "Come To Bossier Shreveport." The K is a requirement for broadcasting stations west of the Mississippi River by the Federal Communications Commission. Steere was also a driving force to encourage the U.S. War Department to bring the Third Attack Wing to Shreveport and Bossier. This venture became Barksdale Field, today's Barksdale Air Force Base.

Among the other neighborhoods he designed and built were Glen Iris, Broadmoor, Dixie Gardens and Hollywood (designed for railroad workers and as an African American residential area).[282] South Highlands is perhaps his most beautiful development. Broadmoor was his most extensive. Two streets—Albert and Steere—are named for him. A.C. Steere Elementary School honors his memory.

A.C. Steere's life reminds us of Edwin Arlington Robinson's 1897 poem "Richard Cory." Both men were fabulously successful, loved, respected and even envied, but that was not enough. Steere was ill for several years, but no one seemed to know his illness was severe. He was still a relatively young man at age fifty, still controlled his businesses and was financially solvent. On Monday, June 30, 1930, Steere gave a party for his employees. The next morning, he said he had insomnia. He went to his bedroom to get dressed and go to work. Instead, he took a pistol, went out to his backyard and shot himself in the heart.[283] The *Shreveport Times* reported the day after he died, "For some time Mr. Steere had been in ill health, suffering from stomach trouble which brought on virtual nervous collapse."[284]

BRUNO AND BERTHA STRAUSS

32°30"02.7261'N 93°43"44.7541'W
B'nai Zion Section in Lots 1A–20A, near southeast corner of Lot 359

STRAUSS
BRUNO   BERTHA BADT
JAN. 14, 1889   DEC. 7, 1885
MAY 22, 1969   FEB. 20, 1970

יה יב יצ ינ ית

The Hebrew inscription translates as
"may his/her/their soul be bound up in the bond of eternal life"[285]

Coming Here As Refugees from Tyranny, They Found
A Haven and a Need That Only They Could Fulfill

The gray granite double monument of Bruno and Bertha Badt Strauss lies near the eastern fence of Greenwood Cemetery in the B'nai Zion section. The plot lies southeast of Lot 359 (the William B. Wiener plot found in this book). The epitaph entices the reader to know more but gives little information of two extraordinary lives and how they came to Shreveport.

Bruno Strauss was born in 1889 in Hannoversch-Münden, Germany. He grew up in Marburg, where his father was a teacher in the Marburg Jewish School and a friend of the philosopher Herman Cohen.[286] Strauss studied

Bruno and Bertha Strauss's double monument. *Image by the author.*

philosophy and German in Marburg from 1906 to 1908 and then at the University of Berlin, where he received his PhD in 1911.[287] He volunteered for German military service in 1915 and served in the Balkans. Before the Great War ended, he accepted a post in Berlin teaching German, Latin and Greek at the Leibniz Gymnasium. He became a professor at Heidelberg University and then taught in Berlin until 1933, when many Jews were dismissed under the Civil Service Restoration Act.[288] Strauss then taught at a private Jewish school before being selected as principal of the Berlin Jewish High School.[289]

The Nazis escalated their intense hatred of Jews during the 1930s, and in August 1939, Bruno and his wife, Bertha, fled their home country with the help of the Emergency Rescue Committee.[290] The couple escaped to London for a short period and then immigrated to the United States, finding a welcoming home at Centenary College in Shreveport, Louisiana. He was a professor of German studies, philosophy and history until his retirement in 1964.[291] Dr. Strauss was an internationally recognized authority on Moses Mendelssohn.[292] Mendelssohn, an eighteenth-century German-Jewish philosopher, was a leader in the Haskalah, the "Jewish Enlightenment."[293] He was also an authority on the writing of his mentor, Hermann Cohen, authoring a three-volume set of his works.[294] Honoring Dr. Strauss on the centennial of his birth, his story was detailed in two major works.[295]

Bertha was also a strident Zionist, as were her brother Herman Badt and her sister Lotte Badt Prager. Bertha's primary focus was the creation of a strong female presence within the Jewish community and a Jewish

Left: Bruno Strauss. *Courtesy of Shannon Glasheen Brock.*

Right: Photo of Bertha Badt Strauss taken in Breslau, circa 1910, at age twenty-five. *Courtesy Jewish Women's Archive.*

Renaissance.[296] She married Bruno Strauss while they lived in Berlin from 1913 to 1921 (except for Bruno's military service during World War I). Bertha fell ill with multiple sclerosis shortly after their son Albrecht was born.[297] She continued to publish at an astonishing pace.

> [She] *published numerous articles in Jewish publications such as the Jüdische Rundschau, Der Jude, the Israelitische Familienblatt, the Blätter des Jüdischen Frauenbundes and Der Morgen, and also in such leading non-Jewish newspapers as the Vossische Zeitung and the Berliner Tageblatt. She co-edited the first scientific edition of Annette von Droste-Hülshoff's works and translated and edited volumes of works by Gertrud Marx, Profiat Duran, Leon da Modena, Süßkind von Trimberg, Heinrich Heine, Rahel Varnhagen, Achim von Arnim, Louise von François, William Rosenau, Fanny Lewald and Moses Mendelssohn. She contributed to the Jüdisches Lexikon and the Encyclopaedia Judaica and wrote short stories, an unpublished biography of Elise Reimarus, an installment novel, a collective biography of Jewish women, and, together with Nachum Tim Gidal, a picture book. Her last editorial work in Germany (together with her husband) was an anthology of letters by Hermann Cohen.*[298]

Her worldview was that of a deeply religious Jew, and she saw life through the lens of German-Jewish life. As the Nazis put an end to written dialogue on race and ethnicity, Bertha's works, like those of all German-Jewish writers, were burned. Their lives were disrupted, and violence was threatened or conducted. Bertha and Bruno escaped less than a month before Germany invaded Poland. Concentration camps operated on a limited basis until then. The Strausses were helped to travel to England and then America. Bruno did not want to move to Palestine because he believed he would not find a job there teaching German history.[299]

Once Bruno and Bertha Strauss settled in Shreveport, she continued her career, really her mission. She wrote articles in prominent publications. Among them were several American-Jewish papers such as the *Aufbau*, *The Jewish Way*, *The Menorah Journal*, *The Reconstructionist*, *The National Jewish Monthly*, the *Hadassah Newsletter* and *Women's League Outlook*.[300] She also published a biography of Jessie Sampter, a noted American Zionist.[301]

WILLIAM DANIEL TOWNSEND

32°30"06.2401'N 93°43"55.1202'W
Confederate Veterans' Bivouac, Lot B

William D Townsend
Co. B
27 Regt
La Inf
CSA
April 12, 1846
Feb. 22, 1953

The Confederate Veterans' Bivouac in Greenwood contains the graves of many men who served in the Confederate States Army. William Daniel Townsend is located in Lot B. Townsend was born in 1846, ran away from home at age sixteen and joined the Confederate army in September 1861.[302] He served as a private in Company B, Twenty-Seventh Louisiana Infantry.[303] The Twenty-Seventh served during the Vicksburg Campaign and acquitted themselves admirably during the battles and Siege of Vicksburg, where Townsend was wounded and almost lost his arm.[304] When Vicksburg fell on July 4, 1863, Townsend, like all other Confederate soldiers inside the fortifications of Vicksburg, was taken prisoner and later paroled. He was just seventeen years old.

Townsend's story includes not only his youthful experience but also his extraordinary longevity. When postwar veterans' organizations in both the North and the South organized, the members retained their service ranks, but as senior members died, the younger men advanced in rank. Over the years, as Townend aged, he was promoted to the rank of general within the United Confederate Veterans (UCV). He was among the last five surviving Confederate veterans of the Civil War.[305] With only one other former Confederate, he attended the final Confederate veterans' reunion in

William Daniel Townsend. *From the* Shreveport Times, *December 27, 1950, 6.*

Norfolk, Virginia, on Memorial Day 1951.[306] He was 105 years old. During his life, Townsend married four times. At the time of his death, his fourth wife, Maggie, was 62. He fathered ten children by his first wife.[307] His first three wives died, and he married Maggie in 1940. The flag at the Louisiana state capitol flew at half-mast, honoring his life and death.[308] When asked about his recipe for a long life, Townsend replied, "The will of the Lord, three tablespoons of whiskey a day and a pipeful of tobacco every 30 minutes."[309]

REVEREND MATTHEW VAN LEAR

32°30″06.1516′N 93°43″54.1532′W
Block 21, Lot 3

Rev. Matthew Van Lear, D.D.
Born In
Williamsport, Md.
April 10, 1837
Died In
Mercer Co. Ky.
June 2, 1903

———

Van Lear
Pastor
Of
First Presbyterian Church
Shreveport from 1887–1901

Lying east of Oleander Avenue across from the Confederate Veterans' Bivouac, in Block 21, Lot 3, is the obelisk of Reverend William Van Lear. Born in Williamsport, Maryland, in April 1837, he became pastor of First Presbyterian Church in Shreveport, serving for fourteen years and retiring in 1901.[310]

Reverend Matthew Van Lear's obelisk. *Image by the author.*

In Lexington, Kentucky, Van Lear attended a synod meeting representing the Transylvania (Kentucky) Presbytery.[311] He died the following year, at age sixty-six, in Mercer County, Kentucky.[312] His family returned his body to Shreveport, where his daughter resided.

Matthew Van Lear's monument is a fine example of a Victorian Egyptian Revival obelisk.[313] Carved of fine white marble, it features an intricate shroud draped over the top and sides with hanging tassels. The obelisk is designed to stand above its neighbors and, in this case, to denote a man of God. The draped shroud illustrates that his life is over but not cut short. The shroud's folds and easy-to-see pyramidal top of the obelisk indicate a long life, well lived.

LUCY VORDENBAUMEN

32°30"05.9473'N 93°43"58.0233'W
Block 36, Lot 5

Our Mother
Lucy Mayo
Beloved Wife Of
E.H. Vordenbaumen
Born at Lake Charles La, 1-9-1864
Died at Shreveport La, 9-18-1903

Located just south of Miriam Avenue and across the street from the Columbarium Pavilion, in Block 36, Lot 5, is a unique monument in Greenwood. The granite monument belongs to the Vordenbaumen family and is dedicated to Lucy Mayo Vordenbaumen. The stone is a diamond-shaped cylinder resting on its lower edge. The upper portion rests on a mid-level base that conforms to the cylinder. The lower platform provides support for the mid-level base. The entire assembly is symbolic of Atlas holding up the world's weight. Although not tall, it can be seen from a distance and stands out among its neighbors. The monument was expensive to create and indicates the family's wealth.

Edward Henry Vordenbaumen was a native of Richmond, Texas. Before arriving in Shreveport in 1896, Vordenbaumen was in the lumber business in Lafayette and New Orleans.[314] He was best known as a principal in the firm

Lucy Vordenbaumen's monument. *Image by the author.*

of Vordenbaumen and Eastman, a large hardware store. Vordenbaumen was active in Shreveport society, publicly minded and served on the City Health Board.[315] Vordenbaumen and Eastman began operations in 1897 at 118 (renumbered to 218) Texas Street and grew beyond the confines of that two-story building the same year.[316] Advertisements in 1897 list the firm as

The Vordenbaumen-Eastham building. *Image by the author.*

"jobbers and dealers in heavy and shelf hardware, plumbers, tinners, mill supplies and agricultural implements."[317]

Lucy Mayo (Vordenbaumen) was born into a wealthy family in Lake Charles, Louisiana, in 1864. She was a socialite and mother to five children.[318] Lucy died following a brief illness at age thirty-nine.[319] E.H. Vordenbaumen remarried but survived his second wife. He died in 1941 after a short illness at age seventy-nine.[320]

Vordenbaumen and Eastham built one of the iconic buildings in downtown Shreveport, the third five-story building in Shreveport, located at 712 Milam Street, also called "Upper Milam."[321] The building features the first commercial elevator in Shreveport, built by Otis. It is large enough to take an entire Conestoga wagon up to the fifth floor for storage or take one down for display.[322]

For many decades, the building was the home to Marcus Furniture, but it is best known for the fading painted sign on its western face. Few people will remember Vordenbaumen and Eastman or Marcus Furniture, but most Shreveporters know it as the "Uneeda Biscuit" building. The ad painted on the west side of the building was part of a national advertising campaign by the National Biscuit Company, better known as NABISCO.

HEWITT HOBSON WHELESS AND ELVIRA SEARCY EAKIN WHELESS

32°30"08.4346'N 93°43"53.3984'W
Masons' Rest, Lot 58

H.H. Wheless
November 21, 1854
June 11, 1912
"By Their Fruits Ye Shall Know Them"
His Wife
Elvira Searcy Eakin
April 6, 1857
June 25, 1918

Near the center of Masons' Rest, in Lot 58, is a grand granite cenotaph that marks the graves of Hewitt Hobson Wheless and his wife, Elvira Searcy Eakin Wheless. H.H. was born in Nashville, Tennessee, in November 1854. He came to Shreveport in 1887 to learn the lumber business. From the mid-1880s to the Great Depression, the United States experienced a great need for good lumber. The Midwest was denuded of virgin forests in the early 1880s, and the South was the last region to possess vast tracts of yellow pine. There was a frenzy to harvest these valuable trees, and the men who controlled the land, the forests, the sawmills and the transportation of the lumber were called "timber barons." Wheless had learned banking in Nashville and brought that knowledge to Shreveport, with a particular

H.H. and Elvira Wheless's cenotaph. *Image by the author.*

knowledge of how industry and banking were intertwined.[323] He partnered with F.T. Whited and built the Whited-Wheless sawmill. The pair owned a substantial stake in the Frost-Johnson Lumber Company and the Allen Manufacturing Company (millwork). He was also a director of the *Shreveport Journal.*

After living in Shreveport for several years, he and his wife, Elvira, moved to Alden Bridge in Bossier Parish to oversee his forty-thousand-acre pine plantation and his large modern sawmill.[324] In effect, Wheless had sold the lumber to himself several years before, and his job in Bossier was to oversee the clearcutting of the trees.

The Wheless family moved back to Shreveport and lived in their mansion at 881 Jordan Street. On the morning of June 11, 1912, Wheless woke up, dressed in his bathrobe and told his family that he would dress and return for breakfast. He went into his bathroom, took a pistol and fatally shot himself in the head.[325] He had been in ill health for some time, according to the *Shreveport Journal*, and he may have suffered from "a nervous strain on account of his physical condition."[326]

At his death, many testimonials provided insight into Wheless. Mayor John Henry Eastham noted, "I feel a keen personal sorrow in this death and am sure this is the universal sentiment, as Mr. Wheless was universally admired." Former governor Newton Crain Blanchard said, "As a businessman, he was wise and clearheaded, seeing many sides and weighing probable results for every proposition submitted to him."[327]

H.H. Wheless's wife, Elvira Searcy Eakin Wheless, was born in Shelbyville, Tennessee, but raised in Arkansas. Her father was a justice of the Arkansas Supreme Court. The couple raised six children, five sons and a daughter. She was a prominent socialite in both Caddo and Bossier Parishes and was particularly active in the United Daughters of the Confederacy and the Daughters of the American Revolution.[328]

In 1918, Mrs. Wheless, age sixty-one, was in declining health. She entered a sanitarium in Battle Creek, Michigan, in May. This was likely the famous Battle Creek Sanitarium, a medical spa managed by Dr. John Harvey Kellogg. Accompanying her were one of her sons, her daughter, her sister and her physician, Dr. M.B. Purnell.[329]

Elvira Wheless died at the sanitarium on June 25, 1918. This brought an enormous outpouring of grief. Reverend James Owens, the former rector at St. Mark's Church in Shreveport, came from New Orleans to conduct the service. Pallbearers at her funeral were F.T. Whited, E.A. Frost, S.B. Hicks, D.B. Hamilton, Dr. M.B. Purnell, Dr. J.L. Scales, W. Beatty Smith, S.J.B. Whited, A.C. Steere, Dr. R.M. Penick and J.H. Arger.[330] Among them were seven timber barons, three physicians and the most prominent real estate developer in the region.

WILLIAM B. WIENER AND SAMUEL GROSS WIENER

32°30″02.8103′N 93°43″44.9840′W
B'nai Zion Section, Lot 359

Shreveport would not be the same today without the extraordinary architecture of the Wiener brothers. Both are buried in the B'nai Zion section of Greenwood. The two men were half brothers. Samuel was born in Shreveport in 1896 and died there in 1977 at age eighty. William was born in Shreveport in 1907 and died there in 1981 at age seventy-four. The brothers were groundbreaking architects, schooled in European and American designs. They designed buildings together and individually. Collectively, they shaped how Shreveport saw itself and how it should be seen. Most of their projects still exist, and several are eligible for the National Register of Historic Places. Among the residences William designed were 641 Longleaf Road, 1050 Ontario Street and 415 Sherwood Road.[331]

Samuel Gross Wiener was a visionary and embodied the International style in many of his projects. He served as the first president of the local chapter of the American Institute of Architects. Among his designs were Airline High School in Bossier City, Arthur Circle Elementary School, B'nai Zion Temple, Bossier High School, the Centenary Amphitheatre, Kings Highway Christian Church, the Coca-Cola Bottling Company in Shreveport, Commercial National Bank, Confederate Memorial Medical Center (now the LSU Health Sciences Center), the science building and women's dormitory at Grambling State University, the terminal at what

Above: William B. Wiener Sr.'s monument. Note the architect's signature. *Image by the author*.

Opposite: William B. Wiener Sr.'s monument close-up. *Image by the author*.

is now Shreveport Downtown Airport, the Shreveport Journal building, the Howard Company Building, the Hunter Building, Linear Junior High School, the Marjorie Lyons Playhouse on the Centenary College campus, the Ricou-Brewster Building, Rubenstein's Department Store, Rusheon Junior High School in Bossier City, the Shreveport Incinerator (now demolished but decades ahead of its time in usefulness, low emissions and aesthetic design), the Washington-Youree Hotel, Werner Park Elementary School and the Wray-Dickinson Building.[332]

William B. Wiener worked in Shreveport for over fifty years and was the senior partner in the firm Wiener, Hill, Morgan, O'Neal, and Sutton. He was a member of the American Institute of Architects and was named a fellow of that organization in 1960 for his achievements in design.[333] Among his designs in Shreveport were the Shreveport Regional Airport; LSU Medical School; several Caddo Parish schools, including J.S. Clarke

Junior High School; B'nai Zion Temple; several homes and churches; and Uptown Shopping Center.[334] Locally, he was involved with the Shreveport Chamber of Commerce, the Shreveport Beautification Foundation and the United Way.[335]

William B. Wiener's grave in the B'nai Zion section, Lot 359, is, by any measure, a unique monument in Greenwood. It hides behind a square hedge that is higher than the average person. Only one entrance marks the plot. Even standing in front of the narrow gap at times, the plot defies entry. Another family monument lies within this whimsical guardian hedge. Once inside, there is no doubt which grave belongs to William B. Wiener.

The monument consists of six slanted granite shafts placed into the ground at an angle. As the visitor moves around this assembly, the shapes change. There are no unpleasing angles. The treat, however, comes when the visitor stands end-on to the stones and realizes that they form a Star of David. The monument was designed by William B. Wiener Jr., a noted architect and sculptor.

These men were giants in their time. Christopher Wren's epitaph in the floor directly under the center of the great dome of St. Paul's Cathedral in London reads, *Si monumentum requiris circumspice*, or "Reader, if you seek his memorial—look around you."[336] This is apropos to the Wiener brothers as well. In 2020, a team of documentary filmmakers created a tribute to the brothers and their works. *Unexpected Modernism* has aired on Louisiana Public Broadcasting, as well as at several venues, and is available on DVD.[337]

DR. JAMES CLINTON WILLIS SR.

32°30"07.1744'N 93°43"54.9704'W
Masons' Rest, Lot 27

Dr. James Clinton Willis Sr., one of the pioneers in Shreveport medicine, lies in Masons' Rest, Lot 27. He was born in Claiborne Parish, Louisiana, in March 1865. He attended Vanderbilt University in Nashville, Tennessee, and graduated from medical school in 1889.[338] Dr. Willis specialized in general surgery, studying at Johns Hopkins University in Baltimore, Maryland, and the Mayo Clinic in Rochester, Minnesota.[339]

Dr. James Clinton Willis Sr.
Willis-Knighton Health System.

He began his medical career in Homer, Louisiana. In 1904, he moved to Shreveport and later joined his friend Dr. J.E. Knighton Sr. in private practice.[340] Dr. Willis became chief of staff at the Shreveport Sanitarium and maintained his private practice.[341] He also served as the chief of the surgical staff at the U.S. Army base hospital in Brownsville, Texas, in 1916 as a member of the Army Reserve Medical Corps. The U.S. Army soon invaded to capture or kill the Mexican guerrilla leader Pancho Villa.[342]

During World War I, Katie Abrams Schroeder, an army nurse, recalled years later that she scrubbed in with Dr. Willis when he performed an emergency appendectomy at a residence. "He was a god! He was a doll!"[343]

Dr. Lewis H. Pirkle and Dr. Thomas E. Williams partnered to create the Tri-State Sanitarium on Greenwood Road in Shreveport in 1924.[344] In 1929, they sold the sanitarium to Dr. Willis, Dr. Knighton and partner doctors J.C. Willis Jr., W.S. Kerlin and Thomas E. Strain. Most of them were from Claiborne Parish and had practiced together.[345] Both doctors Willis and Knighton had sons who shared their names and entered into practice with them. In 1951, long after the retirement of the original doctors Willis and Knighton, the hospital was named Willis-Knighton Memorial Hospital to honor them.[346] Today, Willis-Knighton Health System has five hospitals and multiple clinics serving northwest Louisiana. Dr. Willis died in Rochester, Minnesota, in April 1942 at the age of seventy-seven.[347]

ALEXANDER SMITH WORLEY

32°30″06.1469′N 93°43″55.1143′W
Confederate Veterans' Bivouac, Lot B

A.S. Worley
1 Regt. Butler's Sc Inf CSA
June 8, 1844   Dec 10 1944

Alexander Smith Worley was a Civil War survivor and a gently unreconstructed Rebel. Born in 1844 in Chesterfield, South Carolina, he entered Confederate service as a private in Company F, Forty-Eighth North Carolina Infantry, in the Army of Northern Virginia.[348] During the Battle of Sharpsburg (Antietam), he contracted pneumonia, which may have saved his life. He recovered, returned to North Carolina, reenlisted and was sent to Company C, First South Carolina Infantry Regiment.[349] This unit served as part of the defenses in and near Charleston. He was severely wounded at James Island and lost his right leg below the knee.[350] This injury ended his military career.

He married Caroline Horton in South Carolina in 1872 and fathered three sons.[351] After his wife died, Worley and his three sons moved to Minden, Webster Parish, Louisiana, where he became a schoolteacher.[352] In 1886, he married Frances Rebecca Cronin in Minden. Following Frances's death, he helped raise his grandchildren after his youngest son's wife died

Alexander Smith Worley. *David Hill, Findagrave.*

in 1917. The extended family moved to Keithville in southwestern Caddo Parish and later to Shreveport. One of his granddaughters married a man from Iowa, whom Worley liked. He quipped that he was "a fine gentleman even if he is a stinking Yankee."[353] Later, looking back at his life, he said, "If I have killed a Yankee, I hope God will forgive me. I've even forgiven old [Union general William Tecumseh] Sherman."[354]

The 1940 census lists Worley living with his granddaughter Mary Rippon and her husband, George, on Regent Street in Shreveport.[355] Worley lived to the age of one hundred, dying at the home of his granddaughter, where he lived for the last thirty years of his life.[356] He was the last surviving Confederate of Caddo Parish and the last surviving member of the General Leroy Stafford Camp No. 3 United Confederate Veterans.[357] With his death, northwest Louisiana ended the long chapter with a direct connection to the Civil War.

CHRONOLOGY
OF GREENWOOD CEMETERY

Date	Subject
1871, November 22	"Committee appointed for location new Grave Yard Dec __ 1869." This becomes Alston Cemetery and is a failure.
1893, June 15	Offer of twenty acres from Van Hoose and Tomkies accepted.
1893, October 16	City Council approves plan for surveying the cemetery by Mr. W.B. DeVoe.
1894, January 11	New fence and Potters' Field (first rest) adopted.
1894, January 18	Genevieve Orphanage Rest adopted.
1894, February 13	Confederate Veterans Association Bivouac adopted.
1894, March 8	Fireman's Rest adopted.
1895, July 11	No inside fences are allowed on lots in Greenwood.
1896, June 4	Marble slabs for Potters' Field.
1896, June 4	Knights Templar purchase one acre (beginning of rest).
1897, July 1	More slabs for pauper graves and shed to be constructed.

Date	Subject
1902, March 13	Desecration of graves and removal of flowers from any cemetery prohibited.
1902, September 4	Bid to "furnish coffins and transfer city paupers."
1903, March 16	Independent Order of Odd Fellows purchase Block 37 (rejected).
1903, March 23	"Building and Ground committee ascertain the cost of more territory as a cemetery."
1903, April 20	Knights of Pythias Rest approved.
1903, October 19	A new survey of Greenwood is to be done.
1903, October 23	Monuments for lot corners to be purchased.
1903, November 16	A bid accepted for paupers' graves.
1903, December 21	Cemetery gate erected.
1904, January 26	Fireman's Rest (Lots 3, 4, 5) and survey of Greenwood. Changes made to streets.
1904, April 15	Removal of bodies in the wrong lots.
1904, June 27	Odd Fellows (grading of their acre).
1905, February 27	Bid to supply headstones for pauper graves accepted.
1905, February 27	Advertisement for bids to grade Stoner Avenue up to cemetery gates.
1905, April 25	Permission for wives and children to be buried in the Confederate veterans' section.
1905, April 25	Families allowed to be buried in the Confederate section. Union soldiers allowed "at the option of the General LeRoy Stafford Camp, No. 3."
1905, May 15	Regulations for city cemeteries adopted.
1905, May 15	Copies of ordinance for regulations for city cemeteries to be printed and placed at the cemetery gates.
1905, May 22	Bid awarded for iron fence in front of Greenwood.

Date	Subject
1905, August 8	Marble slabs to be used in pay row, in place of headboards.
1905, September 26	Bithulithic gutters in front of streets with steep grades.
1906, July 16	Curbs and walls around lots in Greenwood and Oakland not to be higher than fifteen inches at any point.
1907, October 8	Building and Grounds recommends looking for a lot of twenty to one hundred acres adjacent to Greenwood
1911, August 22	Knights of Pythias authorized to purchase a triangular piece of ground.
1911, August 22	Mayor authorized to sell a triangular piece of land in Greenwood to Knights of Pythias.
1911, September 12	Authorization to sell property in Greenwood to the Knights of Pythias.
1912, November 26	67.2 acres known as the Fort Humbug tract are authorized for purchase for cemetery purposes.
1915, January 26	Plat of part of Greenwood adjoining Market Street filed; fence to be moved.
1916, January 11	City to donate fifty dollars to the Home for the Homeless to purchase two lots in Greenwood.
1916, January 25	Plat showing the new layout on the east side adopted (Ordinance 2 of 1916).
1917, June 12	Greenwood and Oakland permitted to be used as wild bird sanctuaries.
1925, March 10	Authorization to purchase nineteen acres as an addition.
1925, April 28	Above nineteen acres to be divided into lots to become Greenwood Cemetery II (southeastern quarter of the cemetery).
1925, October 27	Masonic Building Co. to purchase tract in Greenwood Cemetery II.

Date	Subject
1927, June 14	Plots dedicated to American Legion (WWI) and Spanish-American War veterans.
1927, September 13	A portion of Market Street is created from a strip of land in Greenwood.
1927, October 11	Depth of twenty feet added to Spanish-American War veterans' plot (Ordinance 128 of 1927).
1928, February 28	Lot No. 21 Block #77 donated to the "Home for the Aged."
1928, July 10	Ordinance 86 of 1928 introduced: the dedication of Lots 45, 46 and 47 of Block 81 to the Eddington Home for the Aged.
1928, July 24	Dedication of Lots 45, 46 and 47 of Block 81 to the Eddington Home for the Aged (space for sixteen graves).

NOTES

A History and Tour of Greenwood Cemetery

1. See Thomas Bender, "The 'Rural' Cemetery Movement: Urban Travail and the Appeal of Nature," *New England Quarterly* 47, no. 2 (1974): 196–211.
2. Eric J. Brock, *Eric Brock's Shreveport* (Gretna, LA: Pelican Publishing, 2001), 114.
3. U.S. Department of Commerce, 8th Decennial Census (1860), Shreveport and Caddo Parish, Louisiana, unpublished tabulations in the National Archives and Records Administration, Washington, D.C.
4. Map of *Environs of Shreveport and Its Defences, Surveyed by C.U. Lenoir drawn by Lieut. Heilfreich, under direction of Major Venables, Engr. Corps C.S.A.* Known as the Venable Map, copy in the Northwest Louisiana Archives, Louisiana State University Shreveport (LSUS).
5. Ibid.
6. Gary D. Joiner, *Through the Howling Wilderness: The 1864 Red River Campaign and Union Failure in the West* (Knoxville: University of Tennessee Press, 2006), 17–44.
7. Venable Map.
8. Ibid.
9. Contour file (two-foot interval) C_3209327SW.shp found at www.Atlas.LSU.edu.
10. Digital elevation model geographic information system project showing the northern portion of Greenwood Cemetery, Blue Marble Geographics GIS software, cartography by the author.
11. Joiner, *Through the Howling Wilderness*, 185.
12. Shreveport City Council Minutes, Record Book C, 358, December 1869; Book H, 69, April 22, 1871.
13. U.S. Department of Commerce, 9th Decennial Census (1870), Shreveport and Caddo Parish, Louisiana, unpublished tabulations in the National Archives and Records Administration, Washington, D.C.

14. Shreveport, "Listing of the Mayors of Shreveport," www.shreveportla.gov/512/Listing-of-the-Mayors-of-Shreveport.

15. "Confederate Soldiers Who Died at the Confederate and Marine Hospital in Shreveport 1864–1865," in Greenwood Cemetery folder, Northwest Louisiana Archives, LSUS.

16. Eric J. Brock, "Shreveport's Hospitals and Medical Institutions Play a Significant Role in City's History," *Shreveport Times*, June 25, 1994, 15.

17. *Map of Shreveport, Surveyed and Drawn by Wm. R. DeVoe, City Surveyor 1873*, copy in Northwest Louisiana Archives, LSUS.

18. Ibid.

19. Gary D. Joiner and Cheryl White, *Shreveport's Historic Oakland Cemetery: Spirits of Pioneers and Heroes* (Charleston, SC: The History Press, 2015), 149–53.

20. Shreveport City Council Minutes Book F, page 257, Book G, pages 6, 12, 55, 99.

21. Shreveport City Council Minutes Book A, page 368, Book F, page 131, and Book G, page 381.

22. Shreveport City Council Minutes Book G, page 12.

23. Shreveport City Council Minutes Book I, page 89, June 15, 1893.

24. Shreveport City Council Minutes Book I, pages 102, 109, 125, September 28, 1893, October 16, 1893, January 11, 1894.

25. The terms *rest* and *section* are used interchangeably, both in the cemetery and in this book.

26. Shreveport City Council Minutes Book I, pages 102, 109, 125.

27. Shreveport City Council Minutes Book I, page 289, July 11, 1895.

28. Shreveport City Council Minutes Book K, page 279, October 23, 1903.

29. Shreveport City Council Minutes Book K, page 51, May 22, 1905.

30. Shreveport City Council Minutes Book J, page 729, August 4, 1898.

31. Shreveport City Council Minutes Book K, page 43, March 13, 1902.

32. Shreveport City Council Minutes Book K, pages 265–66 and 286, June 12, 1906, and July 16, 1906.

33. Shreveport City Council Minutes Book N, page 310; city of Shreveport Ordinance 38 of 1917, June 12, 1917.

34. All tombs and graves mentioned in this narrative are found in the biographies in this volume.

35. February 18, 1894, donated to the Confederate Veterans Association.

36. Joiner and White, *Shreveport's Historic Oakland Cemetery*, 121–23.

37. Shreveport City Council Minutes Book I, page 127, January 18, 1894. Genevieve is buried in Oakland Cemetery with her parents. The Genevieve Orphanage was located on Olive Street east of Line Avenue.

38. Shreveport City Council Minutes Book N, page 119, January 11, 1916.

39. Shreveport City Council Minutes Book I, page 140, January 26, 1904, March 8, 1894.

40. "Greenwood Cemetery to Dedicate Pavilion, Columbarium," *Shreveport Times*, November 10, 2015.

41. Ibid.

42. Ibid.

43. Shreveport City Council Minutes Book L, pages 365 and 369, August 22, 1911, and September 12, 1911.

44. James R. Carnahan, *Pythian Knighthood: Its History and Literature* (Cincinnati, OH: Pettibone Manufacturing Company, 1892).

45. Shreveport City Council Minutes Book S, page 204–5, October 27, 1925.

46. Douglas Keister, *Stories in Stone: A Field Guide to Cemetery Symbolism and Iconography* (Salt Lake City, UT: Gibbs Smith, 2004), 191.

47. Shreveport City Council Minutes Book K, pages 186 and 429, Book K, March 16, 1903, and June 27, 1904.

48. "In Memoriam," Shreveport 155 newsletter, vol. LX, August 16, 1942, Diamond Anniversary Edition, Northwest Louisiana Archives, LSUS.

49. City of Shreveport, Ordinance 86 of 1928, July 24, 1928.

50. Shreveport City Council Minutes Book T, page 280, February 28, 1928.

51. The Glen, "Our Story," theglen.org/the-glen-our-story; Dr. Ann McLaurin, *The History of the Glen 1898–1998* (Shreveport, LA: Mid-South Press, 1999), 7–26.

52. Shreveport City Council Minutes Book K, page 284, November 16, 1903.

53. Shreveport City Council Minutes Book K, page 361, February 27, 1905.

54. City of Shreveport, Resolution 17, 1928, February 28, 1928.

55. Shreveport City Council Minutes Book K, page 188, March 23, 1903.

56. Shreveport City Council Minutes Book K, page 526, October 8, 1907.

57. Shreveport City Council Minutes Book J, page 85, August 27, 1912.

58. Shreveport City Council Minutes Book M, page 162, November 26, 1912.

59. Shreveport City Council Minutes Book T, page 145; City of Shreveport Ordinance No. 72, June 14, 1927.

60. Shreveport City Council Minutes Book S, page 406; City of Shreveport Ordinance No. 73, June 14, 1927.

61. City of Shreveport Ordinance No. 128, November 128, 1927.

62. Shreveport City Council Minutes Book W, page 67, May 22, 1932.

63. Shreveport City Council Minutes Book W, page 244, May 14, 1935.

64. The foundry mark reads, "Gun 76mm. T124E 2 No. 31. Ord. Corps USA. Wvt Arsenal. 1305 lbs. Insp. H.N.R." The gun was built at the Watervliet Arsenal, near Albany, New York.

65. Shreveport City Council Minutes Book Z, pages 11, 512–13, February 2, 1943.

66. AHEPA, ahepa.org.

67. City of Shreveport City Council Resolution 31 of 1925, March 10, 1925.

68. Stoner Hill Baptist Church, "Stoner Hill Baptist Church History," www.stonerhillbaptistchurch.com/stoner-hill-baptist-church-history.

69. Carpenters, "The UBC Emblem," www.carpenters.org/about-ubc/21st-century-union/the-ubc-emblem.

70. OPCMIA, www.opcmia.org.

71. IUPAT, "About the Union," www.iupat.org/about-us/about-the-union.

72. BAC, bacweb.org.

73. Shreveport City Council Minutes Book V, pages 349–50, June 27, 1932.

Biographies

74. Findagrave.com, "Littleberry Calhoun Allen," www.findagrave.com/memorial/15591441/littleberry-calhoun-allen.

75. "L. Calhoun Allen, Jr.," *Shreveport Journal*, February 25, 1991, 13.

76. Ibid.

77. Conservapedia, "Calhoun Allen," www.conservapedia.com/Calhoun_Allen.

78. For this paragraph, ibid.

79. Ibid.

80. For excellent photos of the original, see History Hit, "Tomb of Cyrus the Great," www.historyhit.com/locations/tomb-of-cyrus-the-great.

81. For this paragraph, see *Biographical and Historical Memoirs of Northwest Louisiana* (Nashville: Southern Publishing Company, 1890), 125.

82. Findagrave.com, "James Walter Atkins," www.findagrave.com/memorial/47290775/james-walter-atkins. Note that the information on Lucille (Lucy) is incorrect. She died in 1922, not 1955. Findagrave.com, "Lucy Atkins," www.findagrave.com/memorial/19454393/lucy-atkins.

83. Keister, *Stories in Stone*, 50.

84. Biographical Dictionary of the United States Congress, "Newton Crain Blanchard," bioguide.congress.gov/search/bio/B000541.

85. National Governors Association, "Gov. Newton Crain Blanchard," www.nga.org/governor/newton-crain-blanchard.

86. "Death of Mrs. N.C. Blanchard," *Shreveport Caucasian*, July 28, 1907, 1.

87. Julliette M. Babbitt, "Some Statesmen's Wives in Washington," *Midland Monthly Magazine* 5, no. 6 (June 1896): 499–506.

88. Findagrave.com, "William Ernest Bland," www.findagrave.com/memorial/46361300/william-ernest-bland.

89. Keister, *Stories in Stone*, 188–89.

90. Woodmen Life, www.woodmenlife.org.

91. Keister, *Stories in Stone*, 189.

92. Ibid., 103.

93. "Ex-Mayor Caldwell Dies at Age of 60: Lung Ailment Proves Fatal to City's Only Three-Time Chief Executive," *Shreveport Times*, August 15, 1953, 1.

94. Ibid., 8.

95. Ibid., 1.

96. "Sam S. Caldwell," *Shreveport Times*, August 16, 1953, 16.

97. Ibid.

98. Ibid.

99. Ibid.

100. *Shreveport Times*, August 15, 1953, 1.

101. Brock, *Eric Brock's Shreveport*, 166.

102. "A Card of Thanks," *Shreveport Journal*, May 27, 1911, 2.

103. "Just as It Happens," *Shreveport Times*, December 11, 1911, 4.

104. "Ida Lee Building Fund: Little Folks Working for New Methodist Church," *Shreveport Journal*, June 24, 1911, 2.

105. *Shreveport Times*, March 17, 1912, 20.

106. Ibid., April 13, 1970, 3.

107. Lilla McLure and J. Ed Howe, *History of Shreveport and Shreveport Builders* (Shreveport, LA: Journal Printing Company, 1937), 257.

108. "Andrew Currie Passes Away after Three Weeks' Illness," *Shreveport Times*, February 9, 1918, 1.

109. Andrew B. Booth, *Records of Louisiana Confederate Soldiers and Louisiana Confederate Commands* (Spartanburg, SC: repr., 1984), 3 vols.

110. *Shreveport Times*, February 9, 1918, 1.

111. "Veterans Pay Tribute to Currie's Memory: Pass Resolutions Commending the Example of His Life and Public Services," *Shreveport Times*, April 16, 1918, 10.

112. Findagrave.com, "Andrew W. Currie," www.findagrave.com/memorial/6919704/andrew-w-currie.

113. These are the St. Paul's Bottoms (Ledbetter Heights) and Allendale neighborhoods west of downtown. They were the first annexations to the city.

114. *Shreveport Times*, February 9, 1918, 1.

115. *Shreveport Journal*, February 11, 1918, 4.

116. Sexton's Report for the Month of June 1907, page 124. The original is located in the Shreve Memorial Library collections.

117. "Touch of Nature," *Shreveport Times*, June 30, 1907, 5.

118. "Succession Notice," *Shreveport Journal*, July 19, 1907, 2.

119. "Succession Notice," *Shreveport Journal*, July 18, 1907, 5.

120. McLure and Howe, *History of Shreveport and Shreveport Builders*, 256.

121. "W.T. Dickinson Dalzell," *Shreveport Times*, February 5, 1899, 1. Most of the information in this section is found in this article.

122. McClure and Howe, *History of Shreveport and Shreveport Builders*, 256.

123. Findagrave.com, "Jean Despujols," www.findagrave.com/memorial/13076220/jean-despujols.

124. "Citizens Honor Mayor's Memory: Dr. S.A. Dickson's Body Lies in State at City Hall," *Shreveport Journal*, June 5, 1916, 12.

125. For full paragraph, ibid.

126. *Shreveport Times*, June 22, 1916, 11.

127. Findagrave.com, "John Henry Eastham," www.findagrave.com/memorial/116208167/john-henry-eastham.

128. See Lucy Vordenbaumen in this volume.

129. Alcée Fortier, *Louisiana: Comprising Sketches of Parishes, Towns, Events, Institutions, and Persons, Arranged in Cyclopedic Form* (Madison, WI: Century Historical Association, 1914), vol. 3, 143–44.

130. Ibid.

131. "Former Mayor, John Eastham, Dies Here," *Shreveport Times*, November 15, 1938.

132. Findagrave.com, "Clarence Heber Ellerbe," www.findagrave.com/memorial/152225879/clarence-heber-ellerbe; and for equipment, Steam Locomotive, "Louisiana Railway & Navigation," www.steamlocomotive.com/locobase.php?country=USA&wheel=4-4-0&railroad=lrn.

133. Findagrave.com, "Clarence Heber Ellerbe."

134. "Clarence Ellerbe," *Monroe Morning World*, August 8, 1937, 1.
135. Findagrave.com, "Cecilia Ellerbe," https://www.findagrave.com/memorial/129302128/cecilia-ellerbe.
136. "Mrs. Cecilia Leonard Ellerbe," *Shreveport Journal*, December 27, 1967, 6.
137. From a traditional Quaker funerary poem. First mention found is from the *Friend's Intelligencer and Journal*, 1890, 538, collection archives (451) at the Pennsylvania State University Library, State College, PA.
138. "Little Girl Dies," *Shreveport Journal*, March 29, 1909, 3.
139. Keister, *Stories in Stone*, 47.
140. Muster Rolls, Third Infantry Regiment, National Archives and Records Administration, Microfilm M378, Roll 11. See also National Park Service, "Gilmore, J.P.," www.nps.gov/civilwar/search-soldiers-detail.htm?soldierId=C39045A1-DC7A-DF11-BF36-B8AC6F5D926A.
141. Ibid. For a thorough history of the Third Louisiana, see Edwin C. Bearss and Willie H. Tunnard, *A Southern Record: The Story of the 3rd Louisiana Infantry, C.S.A.* (Dayton, OH: Morningside Press, 1988).
142. "Died," *Shreveport Times*, May 8, 1900, 4.
143. "Petition," *Daily South-Western*, June 8, 1871, 1.
144. Ibid.
145. "Died," *Shreveport Times*, May 8, 1900, 4.
146. McLure and Howe, *History of Shreveport and Shreveport Builders*, 315.
147. Ibid. The biographical information in this article is found in this source.
148. See photographs by Burch Grabill in the collection of the University of Arkansas–Fayetteville.
149. "Burch E. Grabill, Well-Known Local Photographer, Dies," *Shreveport Journal*, July 1, 1936, 1, 20.
150. Laura Street Connerly, Robert J. Miciotto, Burch Grabill and Bill Grabill, *Photo by Grabill: A Legacy of Images: Burch and Bill Grabill's Northwest Louisiana Archives, Noel Memorial Library, Archives and Special Collections* (Vancouver, WA: Pediment Publishing, 2003).
151. McLure and Howe, *History of Shreveport and Shreveport Builders*, 261.
152. "The Last Roll," *Confederate Veteran* 36 (July 1928): 266.
153. Booth, *Records of Louisiana Confederate Soldiers*.
154. "The Last Roll," 266.
155. Ibid.
156. McLure and Howe, *History of Shreveport and Shreveport Builders*, 261.
157. Ibid.
158. Gary D. Joiner and Ernie Roberson, *Lost Shreveport: Vanishing Scenes from the Red River Valley* (Charleston, SC: The History Press, 2010), 97–110.
159. "The Last Roll," 266.
160. "Major Victor Grosjean," *Shreveport Times*, March 27, 1928, 4.
161. For excellent photos of the original, see History Hit, "Tomb of Cyrus the Great," www.historyhit.com/locations/tomb-of-cyrus-the-great.
162. U.S. Patent No. 504,779, September 12, 1893.

163. Brock, *Eric Brock's Shreveport*, 165; *Torrey et al. v. Hancock*, Circuit Court of Appeals, Eighth Circuit, November 26, 1910, No. 3,311.

164. *Los Angeles Herald*, April 24, 1908, 205.

165. *Estate of Hancock*, 156 Cal. 804 (1909), December 17, 1909, Supreme Court of California, L.A. No. 2425.

166. Brock, *Eric Brock's Shreveport*, 165.

167. Visual inspection of the Hancock tomb with Eric J. Brock prior to his death.

168. "Fair Hardin, Special Prosecutor in State Sift, Is Fearless in His Work," *Shreveport Journal*, August 14, 1939, 3.

169. *Baton Rouge States-Item*, August 11, 1939, 1.

170. "Plaque Is Put Up at Armory: Copper Box Behind It Holds Names of All Men in 204th," *Shreveport Times*, January 10, 1941, 10.

171. "J. Fair Hardin Heads New Organization: Flag Day Observed," *Shreveport Times*, June 15, 1924, 29.

172. "Caddo Chapter D.A.R.," *Shreveport Journal*, December 4, 1929, 14.

173. "Legal Editing Theme of Local Barrister in Address before Club," *Shreveport Journal*, February 11, 1932, 5.

174. "Series of Talks on State Planned: J. Fair Hardin to Give First Address Thursday Night," *Shreveport Journal*, January 31, 1939, 5.

175. J. Fair Hardin, author and ed., *Northwestern Louisiana: A History of the Watershed of the Red River 1714–1937: An Historical Reference Edition Preserving the Record of Growth and Development of the Territory Together with Genealogical and Memorial Records of Its Prominent Families and Personages, Covering the Parishes of Caddo, Bossier, Webster, Claiborne, Lincoln, Jackson, Bienville, Red River, DeSoto, Sabine, Natchitoches, Winn, Grant, and Rapides* (Louisville, KY: Historical Record Association, 1937), 3 vols.

176. "Col. J. Fair Hardin Critically Injured," *Town Talk* [Alexandria, LA], October 29, 1940, 1.

177. "Rites for Col. Hardin Today: Full Military Honors to Be Accorded Deceased National Guard Officer," *Shreveport Journal*, October 31, 1940, 16.

178. For example, *Monroe [LA] New-Star*, October 31, 1940, 7; [Alexandria, LA] *Weekly Town Talk*, November 2, 1940, 6.

179. "Lamented Minister Borne to Last Rest," *Shreveport Times*, July 26, 1914, 8.

180. Ibid.

181. McLure and Howe, *History of Shreveport and Shreveport Builders*, 300.

182. "A Pioneer Preacher Passes," *Shreveport Journal*, July 25, 1914, 4.

183. Findagrave.com, "Robert James Harp," www.findagrave.com/memorial/10626314/robert-james-harp.

184. *Shreveport Times*, July 25, 1914, 12.

185. Ibid., July 26, 1914, 8.

186. "Rev. R.J. Harp, Aged Minister, Is Called Home," *Shreveport Journal*, July 24, 1914, 1.

187. *Shreveport Journal*, July 25, 1914, 4.

188. Ibid.

189. "W.K. Henderson, a Figure in Radio; Stormy Petrel of Southern Broadcasting Dies—Fought Spread of Chain Stores," *New York Times*, May 30, 1945, 19.

190. "W.K. Henderson," *Shreveport Times*, May 30, 1945, 4.

191. For this paragraph, A Dictionary of Louisiana Biography, Louisiana Historical Association, "Henderson, William Kennon," www.lahistory.org/resources/dictionary-louisiana-biography/dictionary-louisiana-biography-h.

192. Ibid.

193. John Schneider, "The Rabble-Rousers of Early Radio Broadcasting," *Radio World* 42, no. 2, 18–20.

194. *Shreveport Times*, May 30, 1945, 4.

195. "Music: KWKH & W.K. Henderson, Jr.," www.caddo.org/98/Parish-History (some articles are not currently accessible).

196. Clifford J. Doerksen, *American Babel: Rogue Radio Broadcasters of the Jazz Age*, American Public Media, americanradioworks.publicradio.org/features/radio/e1.html

197. For this paragraph, "KWKH's 'Hello World' Populist," *Shreveport Journal*, September 16, 1985, 79.

198. Ibid.

199. Ibid.

200. Schneider, "Rabble-Rousers of Early Radio Broadcasting," 18–20.

201. Derek Vaillant, "Bare-Knuckled Broadcasting: Enlisting Manly Respectability and Racial Paternalism in the Battle Against Chain Stores and the Federal Radio Commission on Louisiana's KWKH, 1924–33," *Radio Journal* 3 (2004): 193–211.

202. *Shreveport Times*, May 30, 1945, 4.

203. "A Brief History of Northwest Louisiana Neurosurgery," *Journal of the Louisiana State Medical Society*, March 1, 2020, The Free Library, www.thefreelibrary.com/A+brief+history+of+Northwest+Louisiana+Neurosurgery.-a0238643781.

204. Findagrave.com, "Randell Hunt," www.findagrave.com/memorial/40680078/randell-hunt.

205. Letter from Emily Protho Van Horn, daughter of Virginia Peyre Hunt Prothro, to the author, October 20, 2010.

206. Arkansas Department of Health, Vital Records Section, microfilm for 1904. A great fire destroyed all death records housed in Little Rock for the latter part of 1904 until the beginning of 1914. Theodora's is among the last to survive. CDC, National Center for Health and Statistics, www.cdc.gov/nchs/w2w/arkansas.htm

207. Conversation with Susan Keith, granddaughter of Rhoda Tryon Hunt Keith, January 2022.

208. Possibly a neighborhood or apartment name.

209. Letter in the collection of Susan Keith.

210. "B.K. Jarratt Dies Sunday," *Shreveport Times*, October 30, 1844, 6.

211. Ibid.

212. National Archives and Records Administration (NARA) Microscopy M378, Roll 15.

213. Gary D. Joiner, ed., *Little to Eat and Thin Mud to Drink: Letters, Diaries, and Memoirs from the Red River Campaign, 1863–1864* (Knoxville: University of Tennessee Press, 2007), 1–48.

214. "Brief History of Greenwood Cemetery," Greenwood Cemetery folder, Northwest Louisiana Archives, Noel Memorial Library, LSU-Shreveport.

215. Angola Museum, "1940: The Traveling Electric Chair," www.angolamuseum. org/history-of-angola.

216. Personal conversion with the Honorable Eugene Bryson, former chief judge of the First Judicial District, Caddo Parish, Louisiana.

217. Angola Museum.

218. "Chinese Culture on Menu at Bamboo," *Shreveport Times*, January 26, 1991, 70.

219. Ibid.

220. Ibid.

221. Ibid.

222. Findagrave.com, "Jimmy Jar Poe," www.findagrave.com/ memorial/17758217/jimmy-par-joe.

223. Translation by Dr. Michelle Johns, Department of History and Social Sciences, LSU-Shreveport.

224. Findagrave.com, "David Lefkowitz," www.findagrave.com/ memorial/58412242/david-lefkowitz.

225. Eric J. Brock, "For Half a Century, David Lefkowitz Was 'The Rabbi,'" *Shreveport Times*, March 13, 1991, 9.

226. Ibid.

227. Unless otherwise noted, the remainder of this essay is found in Brock, "For Half a Century."

228. David Lefkowitz Jr., "Freedom Allows True Religion," *Shreveport Times*, September 14, 1987, 46.

229. David Lefkowitz Jr. Papers, Manuscript Collection No. 650, 1943–1990, 12.8 linear feet, Jacob Rader Marcus Center of the American Jewish Archives at Hebrew Union College, Jewish Institute of Religion, Cincinnati, Ohio. collections.americanjewisharchives.org/ms/ms0650/ms0650.html.

230. "Rites for Explosion Victim Here Sunday," *Shreveport Journal*, April 3, 1943, 3; "Eight Killed in Camp Explosion: Lieutenant and Seven Enlisted Men Victims of Demolition Explosion," *Victoria Daily Record* [Vernon, TX], March 31, 1943, 1.

231. Arnold Krammer, *Nazi Prisoners of War in America* (New York: Stein and Day, 1979), 90.

232. "Shreveport Boy Killed in Blast: Pvt. Frank Leonardos and Six Other Victims of Explosion at Camp Swift," *Shreveport Journal*, March 31, 1943, 11; "Former Grid Star Killed in Explosion," *Shreveport Times*, April 1, 1943, 1.

233. LSUHS, "Body Donor Program," www.lsuhs.edu/departments/school-of-graduate-studies/cellular-biology-and-anatomy/body-donor-program.

234. LSUHS, "FAQs about Body Donor Program," www.lsuhs.edu/departments/school-of-graduate-studies/cellular-biology-and-anatomy/body-donor-program/faqs-about-body-donation.

235. Ibid.

236. Findagrave.com, "Samford Brown McCutchen," www.findagrave.com/memorial/10629233/samford-brown-mccutchen.

237. McLure and Howe, *History of Shreveport and Shreveport Builders*, 241.

238. Joiner and Roberson, *Lost Shreveport*, 41–47.

239. Findagrave.com, "Samford Brown McCutchen."

240. "Estate of $236,704 Left by Man and Wife," *Shreveport Journal*, March 19, 1926, 10.

241. Most of the detailed information on Harold Murov is found in his obituary published in the *Shreveport Times*, January 4, 2007.

242. Most of the detailed information on Carolyn Murov is found in her obituary published in the *Shreveport Times*, July 31, 2020.

243. "Martha Segura Nabors," *Shreveport Times*, December 26, 2019.

244. For extensive coverage, see Bernadette J. Polombo, "The Butterfly Man: The Last Murderer Hanged in Shreveport, Louisiana," in Bernadette J. Polombo, Gary D. Joiner, W. Chris Hale and Cheryl H. White, *Wicked Shreveport* (Charleston, SC: The History Press: 2012), 71–84.

245. Ibid., 72.

246. "Slayer Confesses He Is a Fugitive from Georgia Pen," *Shreveport Journal*, April 19, 1934, 1.

247. "The Confession," *Shreveport Journal*, April 18, 1934.

248. "Authorities Use Tear Gas Effectively," *Shreveport Times*, April 18, 1934.

249. "Troops Guard Slayer," *Shreveport Journal*, April 18, 1934.

250. "Jurors Return Guilty Verdict in Minutes," *Shreveport Journal*, April 23, 1934.

251. Ibid.

252. Ibid.

253. Brock, *Eric Brock's Shreveport*, 196.

254. U.S. Department of Commerce, 14th Decennial Census (1920), Shreveport and Caddo Parish, Louisiana, unpublished tabulations in the National Archives and Records Administration, Washington, D.C.

255. U.S. Department of Commerce, 15th Decennial Census (1930), Shreveport and Caddo Parish, Louisiana, unpublished tabulations in the National Archives and Records Administration, Washington, D.C.

256. "Wealthy Shreveport Oil Man Dies of Heart Attack at Chicago," *Shreveport Journal*, July 18, 1940, 1.

257. "R.W. Norton Is Laid to Rest: Rites for Well-Known Oil Man Attended by Throng," *Shreveport Journal*, July 20, 1940, 16; *Chicago Tribune*, July 17, 1940, 1.

258. Information in this paragraph is found in "Gallery Is an Artistic Oasis," *Shreveport Times*, August 7, 1991, 106, and personal visits by the author.

259. "Mrs. Annie Norton," *Shreveport Journal*, March 20, 1975, 12.

260. "Mrs. Annie Miles Norton Dies," *Shreveport Journal*, March 19, 1975, 1.

261. "Services Friday for Mrs. Norton," *Shreveport Times*, March 20, 1975, 9.

262. "Local Woman Saw Service as War Nurse: Mrs. Willa S. Norwood, Here, Served in Spanish American War," *Shreveport Times*, February 6, 1938, 4.

263. *Times-Picayune* Obits, "Lawrence Joseph Planchard," obits.nola.com/us/obituaries/nola/name/lawrence-planchard-obituary?id=15032507.

264. "Nancy Herman Planchard," *Shreveport Times*, August 15, 2011.

265. The Planchard family are close friends of the author and his wife.

266. *Shreveport Times*, August 15, 2011.

267. "Sudden Death: Fireman Mike Roach Succumbs to His Injuries and an Attack of Heart Failure," *Shreveport Times*, February 16, 1899, 5

268. Ibid.

269. Ibid.

270. Ibid.

271. For excellent photos of the original, see History Hit, "Tomb of Cyrus the Great," www.historyhit.com/locations/tomb-of-cyrus-the-great.

272. "A Brief History of Northwest Louisiana Neurosurgery," *Journal of the Louisiana State Medical Society*.

273. "Health Education Is Stressed Here," *Shreveport Journal*, June 27, 1935, 18.

274. Ibid.

275. "Old Hotel First Schumpert," *Shreveport Journal*, October 17, 1966, 34.

276. Christus Health, ChristusHealth.org.

277. Findagrave.com, "Thomas Edgar Schumpert," www.findagrave.com/memorial/7771658/thomas-edgar-schumpert.

278. Keister, *Stories in Stone*, 48.

279. "Honor Memory of Albert C. Steere at Board Meeting," *Shreveport Journal*, July 17, 1930, 18.

280. "Body Discovered in Yard of Home after Shot Fired," *Shreveport Journal*, July 1, 1930, 17.

281. Brock, *Eric Brock's Shreveport*, 131.

282. Ibid., 131–34.

283. For this paragraph, *Shreveport Journal*, July 1, 1930, 17.

284. "A.C. Steere, City Builder, Dies Tuesday," *Shreveport Times*, July 2, 1930, 1.

285. Translation by Dr. Michelle Johns, Department of History and Social Sciences, LSU-Shreveport.

286. Center for Jewish History, Leo Baeck Institute, New York, NY, Bruno Strauss Collection, www.lbi.org.

287. Ibid.

288. Jörg H. Fehrs, *From Heidereutergasse to Roseneck: Jewish Schools in Berlin 1712–1942* (Berlin: Hentrich, 1993), 279–81.

289. Ibid.

290. Findagrave.com, "Bruno Strauss," www.findagrave.com/memorial/45849412/bruno-strauss.

291. Eric J. Brock, *Centenary College of Louisiana* (Charleston, SC: Arcadia Publishing, 2000), 113.

292. Bruno Strauss, ed., *Moses Mendelssohn: Collected Writings* (Jubilee Edition), vol. 11, *Correspondence I (1754–1762)* (Stuttgar-Bad Cannstatt, 1974).

293. Stanford Encyclopedia of Philosophy, "Moses Mendelssohn," plato.stanford. edu/entries/Mendelssohn.

294. Bruno Strauss, ed., *Hermann Cohen's Jewish Writings*, 3 vols. (Berlin: Schwetschke, 1924); Hermann Cohen, *Religion of Reason from the Sources of Judaism*, revised from the author's manuscript and provided with an afterword by Bruno Strauss (Frankfurt am Main: J. Kauffmann, 1929); Herman Cohen, *Letters, Selected and Edited by Bertha and Bruno Strauss* (Berlin: Salman Schocken, 1939).

295. Joseph Walk, ed., *Short Biographies on the History of the Jews 1918–1945* (Jerusalem: Leo Baeck Institute, 1988), 358; Barbara Händler-Lachmann, "…that this young man doesn't have to shy away from prejudice and distrust towards us: Bruno Strauss on his 100th Birthday" (Marburg, Germany: Studier' mal Marburg, 1989), vol. 14, 19–20.

296. See Martina Steer, *Bertha Badt-Strauss (1885–1970). Eine jüdische Publizistin* (Frankfurt/Main: Campus Verlag, 2005).

297. Martina Steer, "Bertha Badt-Strauss," Jewish Women's Archive.

298. Ibid.

299. Ibid.; see also Barbara Hahn, "Bertha Badt-Strauss (1885–1970), *Die Lust am Unzeitgemäßen*," in *Frauen in den Kulturwissenschaften* (Munich: C.H. Beck, 1994), 152–64.

300. Ibid.

301. Bertha Strauss, *White Fire: The Life and Works of Jessie Sampter* (New York: Reconstructionist Press, 1956).

302. "104-Year Old Confederate Veteran Visits Shreveport," *Shreveport Times*, December 27, 1950, 6.

303. Muster Roll, 27th Louisiana Infantry Regiment, National Archives and Records Administration, Microfilm M378, Roll 29. See also National Park Service, "Townsend, W.," www.nps.gov/civilwar/search-soldiers-detail. htm?soldierId=43DA28DA-DC7A-DF11-BF36-B8AC6F5D926A.

304. For a full account of the 27th Louisiana Infantry, see Allan C. Richard Jr. and Mary Margaret Higginbotham Richard, *The Defense of Vicksburg: A Louisiana Chronicle* (College Station: Texas A&M Press, 2004); "Hemorrhage Fatal to 'Uncle Eli' in Olla: State's Last Civil War Veteran, William Townsend, Dies at 106," *Shreveport Times*, February 23, 1952, 1.

305. "Civil War Vet Dies: William Townsend, 106, Was One of 5 Confederate Survivors," *Providence* [RI] *Journal*, February 23, 1953, 1.

306. "Two Old Vets at Convention: William D. Townsend of Olla Is One of Pair Attending," *Monroe News-Star*, May 30, 1951, 1.

307. "Hemorrhage Fatal to 'Uncle Eli,'" 1.

308. "Capitol Flag at Half Mast for La. Confederate Vet," *Shreveport Times*, February 24, 1953, 7.

309. Ibid.

310. "A Beautiful Bride of Yesterday," *Shreveport Journal*, March 12, 1935, 6.

311. "Synod Meeting: Southern Branch of Presbyterian Church in Session Here Today," *Lexington* [KY] *Herald-Leader*, October 14, 1902, 5.
312. Findagrave.com, "Matthew Van Lear," www.findagrave.com/memorial/6919413/matthew-van_lear.
313. Keister, *Stories in Stone*, 16.
314. "Death Takes Old Resident: E.H. Vordenbaumen Dies in Local Sanitarium: Service Today," *Shreveport Times*, December 14, 1941, 26.
315. "City Health Board Held Busy Session," *Shreveport Journal*, January 12, 1911, 6.
316. "For Rent," *Shreveport Times*, July 24, 1897, 8.
317. Advertisement, *Shreveport Sunday Judge*, February 14, 1897, 1.
318. Obituary, *Shreveport Journal*, September 20, 1903, 2.
319. "Society," *Shreveport Times*, September 27, 1903, 16; Findagrave.com, "Edward Henry Vordenbaumen," www.findagrave.com/memorial/78221228/edward-henry-vordenbaumen.
320. Findagrave.com, "Edward Henry Vordenbaumen."
321. "Big Buildings to Be Erected," *Shreveport Journal*, May 8, 1902, 1.
322. Joiner and Roberson, *Lost Shreveport*, 76.
323. "The Death of a Prominent Shreveporter," *Shreveport Journal*, June 11, 1912, 1.
324. Ibid.
325. Ibid.
326. Ibid.
327. "Wheless: Funeral Serviced in City," *Shreveport Journal*, June 12, 1912, 6.
328. "Mrs. Wheless's Funeral Here," *Shreveport Times*, June 26, 1918, 2.
329. "Just As It Happens," *Shreveport Times*, May 12, 1918, 18.
330. "Rev. James Owens to Come from New Orleans for Wheless Funeral: City's Most Prominent Men to Act as Pallbearers of Well Known Woman," *Shreveport Journal*, June 26, 1918.
331. "A Louisiana Trust for Historic Preservation Fundraising Ramble," *Shreveport Times*, October 19, 2015, A6.
332. Findagrave.com, "Samuel Gross Wiener," www.findagrave.com/memorial/71886774/samuel-gross-wiener.
333. "William B. Wiener, Shreveport Architect, Dies," *Shreveport Times*, January 8, 1981, 10.
334. Ibid.
335. "Well Known Local Architect William Wiener Dies at 74," *Shreveport Journal*, January 7, 1981, 14; Findagrave.com, "William Benjamin Wiener," www.findagrave.com/memorial/45812962/william-benjamin-wiener.
336. Explore St. Paul's Cathedral, www.explore-stpauls.net/oct03/textMM/WrensTombN.htm.
337. www.lpb.org/shop/items/unexpected-modernism-dvd; Unexpected Modernism, unexpectedmodernism.com.
338. Willis-Knighton Talbot Medical Museum, "Dr. James C. Willis, Sr. Biography 1865–1942," museum.wkhs.com/collections/online-collections/details/dr.-james-c.-willis-sr.-1865-1942.

339. Ibid.
340. Ibid.
341. *Shreveport Times*, July 16, 1905, 8.
342. "Louisiana Men Well Located," *Shreveport Times*, July 28, 1916, 1.
343. "She Talks of Days When 'Nursing…Was Nursing," *Shreveport Times*, October 6, 1989, 4.
344. James K. Elrod, *Bread Crumbs to Cheesecake* (Shreveport, LA: R&R Publishers, 2013), 15–17.
345. Ibid., 21–22.
346. "Hospital Name Is Changed to Honor Two Physicians," *Shreveport Times*, January 20, 1952, 10.
347. Findagrave.com, "James Clinton Willis," www.findagrave.com/memorial/107266499/james-clinton-willis.
348. Muster Roll, 48th North Carolina Infantry Regiment, National Archives and Records Administration, Microfilm M230, Roll 43. See also National Park Service, "Worley, Alexander," www.nps.gov/civilwar/search-soldiers-detail.htm?soldierId=5A7C06E1-DC7A-DF11-BF36-B8AC6F5D926A.
349. Ibid.
350. Ibid.
351. Eric Brock, "Presence of the Past: Shreveport's Last Four Confederates," *Shreveport Times*, July 22, 1995, 16.
352. Ibid.
353. Ibid.
354. Ibid.
355. U.S. Department of Commerce, 16th Decennial Census (1940), Shreveport and Caddo Parish, Louisiana, unpublished tabulations in the National Archives and Records Administration, Washington, D.C.
356. "Civil War Vet Dies Saturday: A.S. Worley Reached Age 100; Funeral on Monday," *Shreveport Journal*, December 30, 1944, 2; "100 Year-Old Veteran, A.S. Worley, Dies," *Shreveport Times*, December 31, 1944, 10.
357. "Alexander Smith Worley Lay on Battlefield in 1864 with Water Dripping from Bucket on Wound," *Shreveport Times*, December 31, 1944, 1.

ABOUT THE AUTHOR

Gary D. Joiner received a BA in history and geography from Louisiana Tech University, an MA in history from Louisiana Tech University and a PhD in history from St. Martin's College, Lancaster University, in the United Kingdom. He is a professor of history and chair of the Department of History and Social Sciences at Louisiana State University in Shreveport, where he holds the Mary Anne and Leonard Selber Professorship in History and serves as chair of the Department of History and Social Sciences, the director of the Strategy Alternatives Consortium and director of the Red River Regional Studies Center.

He is the author, co-author or editor of thirty-seven books, including *9/11: A Remembrance*; *Operation Senior Surprise: The Secret Squirrels and the Opening of Operation Desert Storm*; *Deterrence: A Brief History and a Case Study in Cold War Practice*, part I: *1945–1953*, *Operation Linebacker*, part II, *A Remembrance*; *Henry Chilvers: Admired by All*; *History Matters*; *Shiloh and the Western Campaign of 1862*; *One Damn Blunder from Beginning to End*; *Through the Howling Wilderness*; *No Pardons to Ask Nor Apologies to Make*; *Little to Eat and Thin Mud to Drink*; *Mr. Lincoln's Brown Water Navy*; *Red River Steamboats*; *Historic Shreveport-Bossier*; *Lost Shreveport: Vanishing Scenes from the Red River Valley*; *Historic Haunts of Shreveport*; *Wicked Shreveport*; *Historic Oakland Cemetery*; *Local Legends of Shreveport*; *Red River Campaign: The Union's Last Attempt to Invade Texas*; and *The Battle of New Orleans: A Bicentennial Tribute*. Dr. Joiner is also the author of numerous articles and technical reports and served as a consultant for ABC, CBS, Fox News, PBS, the Associated Press, A&E Network, C-SPAN, the Discovery Network, HGTV, the History Channel, MSNBC, SyFy and MTV, among others.

Visit us at
www.historypress.com
···